WE GAVE AWAY A FORTUNE

STORIES OF PEOPLE WHO HAVE DEVOTED THEMSELVES AND THEIR WEALTH TO PEACE, JUSTICE AND THE ENVIRONMENT

Christopher Mogil and Anne Slepian with Peter Woodrow
Illustrated by Yani Batteau

NEW SOCIETY PUBLISHERS
PHILADELPHIA, PA   GABRIOLA ISLAND, BC

PUBLISHED IN CO-OPERATION WITH THE FUNDING EXCHANGE

Inquiries regarding requests to reprint all or part of *We Gave Away a Fortune: Stories of People Who Have Devoted Themselves and Their Wealth to Peace, Justice and the Environment* should be addressed to:
New Society Publishers
4527 Springfield Avenue
Philadelphia, PA 19143

ISBN USA 0-86571-220-4 Hardcover
ISBN USA 0-86571-221-2 Paperback
ISBN CAN 1-55092-166-5 Hardcover
ISBN CAN 1-55092-167-3 Paperback

Printed in the United States of America on partially recycled paper by Capital City Press of Montpelier, Vermont.

Cover photograph by Impact Visuals.
Cover design by g.e. jarrett.
Book design by Martin Kelley.

To order directly from the publisher, add $2.50 to the price for the first copy, 75¢ each additional. Send check or money order to:
New Society Publishers
4527 Springfield Avenue
Philadelphia, PA 19143
In Canada, contact:
New Society Publishers/New Catalyst
PO Box 189
Gabriola Island, BC VOR 1XO

Published in co-operation with The Funding Exchange.

New Society Publishers is a project of the New Society Educational Foundation, a nonprofit, tax-exempt, public foundation. Opinions expressed in this book do not necessarily represent positions of the New Society Educational Foundation.

® GCU

DEDICATION

To those wealthy people of the world who are liberating themselves
from the gilded cage, discovering the immeasurable fulfillment
of sharing the earth with a diverse and precious human family,
and joyfully helping to create a world
where each of us is assured an ample share of what we need.

TABLE OF CONTENTS

Prologue vii
Introduction 1

STORIES

Millard Fuller 5
Edorah Frazer 9
Sallie Bingham 15
Joe Collins 19

THE POLITICAL AND SOCIAL CONTEXT

Giving It Away 25
What's My Fair Share? 29
Liberation for the Rich 38
Building Security 43

STORIES

Charles Gray 49
Nelia Sargent 54
Chuck Collins 59
Joe and Terry Havens 65

PERSONAL ISSUES ABOUT WEALTH

Beyond Guilt and Shame 71
Revealing Ourselves as Wealthy 76
Families and Money 81
Finding Meaningful Work 86

STORIES

Ben Cohen 91
John Steiner 95
Betsy Duren 99
Robbie Gamble and Martha Miller 104

TAKING PART IN THE WORLD

Sharing Power and Privilege 109
Spiritual Economics 114
Our Giving Makes a Difference 120
Doing a Lot with a Little 125

STORIES

Tracy Gary 131
Phil Villers 138
George Pillsbury 143
Ram Dass 148

APPENDICES

Questions for Reflection 154
Exercises: Class Background, Class Spectrum Chart 158
A Spectrum of Current Class Groups in the U.S. 160
Financial Timeline 162
Thumbnail Biographies of Other Interviewees 164
Annotated Bibliography 169
Resource List 174
Support for Making Change 178

PROLOGUE

Let me confide a secret: I have a lot of money.

One day in 1978, I got a call from a woman who identified herself as the secretary of my stock broker. "Don't hesitate to ask us if you have any questions about your portfolio," she told me. "What are you talking about?" I asked. This is how I discovered that I had just received an inheritance from my grandmother.

I was shocked and excited. No one in my family had ever told me that my grandparents would leave me a lot of money. I also felt embarrassed at my sudden wealth. At the time I was living on a meager income with a community of social change activists in West Philadelphia.

The more I pondered, the more conflicted I felt. I could do anything I wanted with this money. Given my modest lifestyle, I no longer had to work for a living. Yet why should I be wealthy when most other people were not? Should I spend the money on myself, or help make life easier for my friends? Should I use it to promote a better world? How could I take care of this money so as not to lose it? My head whirled with questions.

Unsure of how to use my new-found wealth I began experimenting. I gave the first $2,000 to help a group I worked with, and another few thousand to a social change foundation. Over the next few years, I gave away between a third and a half of my annual net income from investments, while I lived on the rest. Eventually, I began to ask myself why I did not give substantially more. I was reluctant — in fact, on closer examination, afraid — to give away "too much." I was becoming attached to the freedom to explore work I felt called to do without having to work "for a living."

I was haunted by the question of why I should have this privilege. I wondered whether I was simply being selfish, pampering myself and avoiding my own insecurities about working. At bottom was a fairly simple question: should I give away my wealth?

I needed someone to talk with, but discovered that most people just do not discuss their personal finances, and I, too, joined the polite silence. I did not say to my family members, "I hope you don't mind my asking, but I'm curious: how did you spend your money last year?" or "By the way, how much do you give away?" I knew those questions would be too threatening, to them and to me.

Then I learned about a network of progressive, wealthy people who get together once a year to talk about what it's like to believe in equality and democracy and yet control lots more resources than most people. Over the next few years I went to a number of these conferences, organized by Haymarket People's Fund in Boston and by The Funding Exchange in New York. For the first time, I was able to talk openly about money issues. But the discussion always seemed limited to how to invest our assets and give away only small portions of our income. People evidently assumed we were supposed to keep all our assets. Maybe that was the most sensible choice, but it seemed peculiar to me that at over a dozen conferences about money and giving, no one raised the topic of giving away principal.

Then in the spring of 1986, a woman at a Haymarket conference boldly asked the group, "Has any of us seriously considered giving away our wealth?" There was stunned silence, except for my pounding heart. I raised my hand, and was excited to see a few others raise theirs also. Four of us met that afternoon to share our stories. We were so excited to be finally discussing our desires and fears about wealth, we decided to continue to meet. We explored the pros and cons of giving away principal; whom to involve in major money decisions; how to communicate with our families about money; and what criteria to use in funding decisions. We felt buoyed by these discussions, but as we grew more serious about giving away a chunk of our assets we grew uneasy. Would others who had given away their wealth tell us grisly tales of naive generosity followed by bitterness and regret? We wanted to talk with others who had already done what we were contemplating — to learn how they had decided and how they felt about it afterwards — to avoid repeating their mistakes.

So we became amateur detectives. How do you find rich people who have given a lot of their assets to social change? They don't advertise themselves — there is no club, no professional association. We began looking for contacts. We called people we knew who were connected to foundations. We talked with a reporter from the New York Times and a researcher on philanthropy at Boston College. Little by little, we found and interviewed a few people who had given away assets. Word of the project spread and others began referring people to us. Over four years, we talked with 40 people, each of whom had given away assets, ranging from hundreds of thousands to tens of millions of dollars. To our surprise, we found no disaster stories, only inspiring and thought-provoking experiences from people who were living happily and with integrity. In a culture unabashed in its emphasis on consumption and profit-making, these people reassured us that it was possible to live according to our values, and that we might well feel richer for doing so.

Thus fortified, members of our group gave away some of their wealth. Edorah gave away 80% of her inheritance, Chuck nearly all of his. I decided (with my grandfather's approval) to set up a small foundation — the "Chutzpah Fund" — with all the money he was planning to leave me. Nancy, single and with health problems, decided to retain her assets, investing most of them into low-interest housing loans that would benefit low-income people in the community.

Whenever we talked to friends about our interview project they would ask when they could buy the book. We hadn't planned to write a book! However, enough people wanted it that we committed ourselves to the project. Together we interviewed more donors and defined the key issues, and then I spent countless hours glued to the computer. With lots of help from my friends, this book was born.

This project has given me valuable insights into how to live a life that honors being part of humanity and the planet Earth, a life that truly nourishes me. I feel less judgmental towards others and myself about how to use money — and more flexible about how to live with passion and purpose. After years of uneasily grappling with the question "What's my fair share?" I feel relaxed and blessed by the resources I have to offer. I don't feel I have "given up" anything. I enjoy, instead, a pleasure akin to having given a special gift to a loved one, a feeling of being enriched and strengthened by taking part in something larger than myself.

— Christopher Mogil

ACKNOWLEDGMENTS

When we glance at acknowledgments in non-fiction books, we are always flabbergasted by the army of people thanked. From our own experience we've discovered that our own generous and attentive army was indispensable to emerging from years of staring at a computer screen to handing a manuscript to the publisher.

We gratefully acknowledge many friends and associates for their significant contributions to this book: Chuck Collins, Edorah Frazer and Nancy Brigham, for helping launch the project, for ongoing support, and for sharing in the greater adventure with courage and humor; Peter Woodrow for distilling and organizing ideas, Dakota Butterfield for her colorful editing and unabashed enthusiasm, John Lapham and Yani Batteau for their creative work on the illustrations and Richard Curran for his charts; Jerry Koch-Gonzalez for his unflagging visionary assistance; Debbie Friedman for her consistent support, and Shelly Kellman, Melissa Everett, Charlie Varon, Ann Doley, and Peter Solomon for thoughtful editorial help and encouragement. We appreciate the interest and thoughtful input of Greg Bates, Marcie Boyd, Joanie Bronfman, Steve Chase, Ellen Deacon, Robert Dove, Betsy Duren, Sara Elinoff, Alexander Gauguine, Helena Halperin, Annie Hoffman, Robert Irwin, Michael Jaro, Rob Kanzer, Sue Kranz, Dennis Pearne, Johnn Prance, Helena Reilly, Venita Robertson, John Rosario, Paul Schervish, Eric Segal, Jan Slepian, Stephanie Smith, Steve Wineman, Jean Weiss, Anne Wright, Betsy Wright, Felice Yeskel, and Jane Yett.

We thank the Institute for Community Economics, as well as June Makela, Ann Doley, Jackie Schad, and The Funding Exchange for backing the project; and T.L. Hill and David Albert at New Society Publishers for their assistance in the project; and the CPF clip-art service for illustration ideas. We were encouraged by the staff and donor community of Haymarket People's Fund, The Funding Exchange and its member community funds, and members of the Threshold Foundation community.

Most of all, we wish to acknowledge the people who share their stories here, without whose courage, generosity, and openness this project would have been an idle dream.

INTRODUCTION

"Never before have so many people stood to inherit so much," announced the *U.S. News & World Report* in its May 7, 1990 issue.[1] Over $8 trillion — the personal net worth of Americans over 50 — will soon pass to a younger generation. The article concludes: "While only some baby-boomers will receive that money, all will inherit a legacy of serious problems that their parents couldn't or wouldn't solve ... The largest issue for the baby-boomers who cash in on the boom is whether they will think it wise or necessary to share some of their good fortune."

The following pages describe the lives and issues of people who were moved to share their "good fortune" by committing themselves and their wealth to promote peace and social justice. They are people who wrestled with questions such as: What do I do as a privileged person pained by the state of the world? How can those of us who have more, share with those who have less? How can we live our lives true to the relationships we desire with others in our global family?

Most people in our society do share their money — to some degree. People commonly give from 1-3% of their income to support causes or religious organizations. It is rare and considered generous to give 10% of one's income; and to give 50% or more is extraordinary. Most people seek to *become* wealthy, not to give their money away! For example, in Massachusetts, in any given month, 60% of all adults play the lottery, and when the jackpot is big, 80-90% of the adults in the state pay for the enticing fantasy of striking it rich.[2,3]

Even wealthy people who write substantial checks to charity usually give just a modest percentage of their income from investments. The individuals we interviewed were strikingly different. Not only did they give away sizeable amounts: they gave well beyond their investment income. They gave away a substantial part of the "fortune" itself — the financial principal.

"Principal" is the bulk of one's financial assets. When invested the principal brings interest, dividends, or rent — unearned income. The unearned income is often reinvested... at which point it becomes more principal... which earns more money ... and thus total wealth multiplies. (Also, if stock or real estate values go up, the principal itself increases in value, sometimes by a great deal.) In most well-to-do families, the Eleventh Commandment is "Thou Shall Not Invade Thy Principal." The unquestioned assumption is that principal should be invested wisely and passed down to children and grandchildren. So by giving away substantial portions of their principal, the people we interviewed violated one of the most sacred taboos in the world of the wealthy, a core precept unquestioningly followed by monied families and the financial professionals who work for them.

How much of their principal did these people give? We sought people who had given at least $100,000, but more significantly, who had given away at least 20% of their total assets. (Because it is unusual for investments to average consistently 20% per year, giving 20% means delving into principal as well as income.) As it happened, many of those we interviewed gave away over 50% of their principal, and several gave away all or nearly all of their wealth.

We were looking for another special characteristic in the givers we sought to interview. We sought people who had used their wealth and their lives to help change the underlying structures in society that create injustice.

This is quite different from traditional philanthropy. Many wealthy people write sizeable checks — but usually to support private schools and colleges, symphonies, opera houses, and other institutions that benefit the wealthy far more than the poor. Even when people intend their contributions to "help the disadvantaged," they usually give to traditional charities that leave the underlying causes of social problems untouched. Certainly, the lessening of suffering is worthwhile — creating food pantries for the hungry, building shelters for the homeless. But if the conditions which create poverty are left unchanged, for every person fed or housed, thousands more become hungry or homeless. In contrast, social change philanthropy aims to change the political, economic, and social structures which create the problems in the first place. This usually means supporting the efforts of people to organize and empower themselves, to fight for greater rights and economic and political participation.

As special as these givers are, we imagine there are hundreds more wealthy people who have quietly directed over 20% of their principal annually to social change. Presented here are the stories of 40 such people — 13 women and 27 men (not counting spouses), all white, ranging in age from 25 to 77. They represent a range of professions — school teachers, publishers, activists, writers, business entrepreneurs, parents, and homemakers, among others — and a range of ways to give money and energy to promote social change.

For example, Phil Villers used half his fortune ($40 million) to establish a foundation to support advocacy for the elderly. Charles Gray gave away all his money to live simply, to promote a model of equitable living, and work for the poor and homeless. Betsy Duren gave her money to a foundation specializing in funding grassroots peace groups, and today works as a consultant with such groups. Ben Cohen, who gave about $500,000 of his company stock to launch the Ben and Jerry's Foundation, uses his job flexibility and influence to work for peace and corporate responsibility.

We were excited to meet with these people who had given not only their money but their time, their talents, and their passion to the work of creating a more equitable world. Remarkably, not a single one of them regretted the decision to give away their wealth. The stories they told challenged our stereotypes about wealthy people and helped us think creatively about how those who have wealth can be catalysts and participants in efforts for economic justice.

*   *   *   *   *

A few words about how we set up the book:

Most of the book is personal interviews. Many of those we interviewed are "going public" about their giving for the first time. In fact, for some, telling their story to us was the first time they told it to anyone. Most of the interviews were done in a single visit of an hour or two, and some were just by phone — not a lot of time to develop trust. They were naturally protective of others they mentioned in their stories, not wanting to expose family members or friends, so sometimes just a few words hint at important issues people struggled with for years. Still, most of the interviews we have included are remarkably frank and detailed.

Between the clusters of stories, we highlight common themes to provide a social, political, and spiritual context for the actions and choices of these individuals. In these theme chapters we generalize not only from the interviews, but also from our personal and professional experiences of years of working with wealthy people.

We assume that not everyone will read the book from beginning to end, so each chapter stands on its own to allow dipping into whatever stories and themes spark a reader's interest.

Only 16 full interviews appear in the text: thumbnail sketches of our other interviewees appear in the Appendices. If a quote is credited to people with no footnote after the names, they are additional interviewees. Where people preferred to remain anonymous, their pseudonyms appear in quotes (for instance "Penny Lippincott").

Take a look at the Appendices: Browse through the bibliography and resource list to see what's useful, and try out the exercises and questions for reflection. The questions are organized by theme chapters.

*   *   *   *   *

We wrote this book especially for people who have surplus resources, who want to contribute meaningfully to changing the world, and who seek to have their daily lives reflect more of their deepest values. For those who feel nervous about giving more, but whose hearts call out to do so, we offer this book as a source of inspiration and as a guide. If you are wealthy but never considered giving to social change, we hope you will relate the themes we explore to your life, and enjoy the process of questioning your relationship to money and giving.

What follows here is not meant to convince the unconvinced, or to change the minds of those who see the world very differently. Books with detailed political arguments and documentation of social ills are in the bibliography and endnotes; in our discussions, we assume agreement with a basically progressive perspective.

Nevertheless, we hope these stories will find their way to people from many different economic backgrounds and political persuasions. If you consider yourself not rich, but "decently comfortable," or "getting by," this book may reveal how rich you really are in global terms, and what you can do with what you have. If you are struggling to make ends meet, we hope you will be intrigued and encouraged by this portrayal of people in very different circumstances and how the class system affects them. If you are concerned with building alliances across classes, we hope this book will offer insight that will prove useful in your work.

Whatever your economic situation, we hope the stories that follow will give fresh insight into the meaning of wealth. Accept the following stories and theme discussions as a gift, to help acknowledge your full wealth and use all of it — money, talents, skills, and life energy — to further your most heart-felt values and dreams.

1. Paul Glastris et al., "Baby Boomers Hit the Inheritance Jackpot," *U.S News & World Report*, May 7, 1990.

2. From David Ellis of the Massachusetts State Lottery, June 4, 1991.

3. We say "the enticing fantasy of striking it rich" because the chances of winning a big jackpot are between 2 and 14 million to one, depending on the game and the state. "You are considerably *more likely* to die from lightning (about 2 million to 1), in a car crash (about 6,000 to 1), syphilis (about 1 million to 1), or from a falling object (about 15 times more likely according to National Center for Health Statistics) than you are of winning the lottery." From Wagman, Robert. *Instant Millionaires: Cashing in on America's Lotteries.* Washington, D.C.: Woodbine House, 1986.

MILLARD FULLER

In 1976, a decade after giving away his earned wealth, Millard founded Habitat for Humanity, an international network of organizations building housing "for God's people in need." He now travels extensively, talking about the power of "biblical economics" and building the Habitat movement.

My dad came from a poor family. When he was 18 years old, his father was disabled by rheumatoid arthritis. My dad went to work and did not even get to finish high school until he was 25 years old, because he was supporting the family. He eventually started working for a cotton mill in Alabama, and worked his way up to being a manager. After that he decided to go into business for himself and opened a small grocery store and then a soft ice cream establishment. He made quite a bit of money. With the money he bought a 400-acre farm and went into the cattle business.

I was raised by a dad who was doing well in business, so he got me into business. I got caught up into making money and went off to college, where I formed a business with a fellow student. Over an eight-year period, the business grew and mushroomed and made incredible money.

Then, in November 1965, my wife left me. My wife and children were very important to me, but I pretty much took them for granted — until I saw I was about to lose them. I pursued my wife to New York and convinced her we could start a new life. We agreed that I would leave the business and donate all of our money to charitable causes. We didn't sit around and ponder for weeks about the advantages of keeping the money and the advantages of giving it away; it was a decision that we made very quickly.

My business partner and I owned over 2,000 acres of land and hundreds of head of cattle and horses. We had fishing lakes, two speedboats, and a cabin on the lake. We had everything that money could buy: Lincoln Continental, a beautiful home in the Cloverdale section of Montgomery, and a 20-acre lot for which we had already drawn plans for a $150,000 house — in the dollars of over 20 years ago! We got rid of all of it. We sold it and gave away all of the money. I have never regretted it — it was one of the wisest things that I ever did.

I am a Christian person, fired and motivated by the Christian faith, and I feel that it was divine guidance that caused me to take this step. I feel strongly that material abundance was getting in the way of my family relationships and my spiritual life, and that attachment to material things was what got me into trouble. Giving it all away was a dramatic, radical step, one which society might consider somewhat foolish, but I was raised in the Church and have done a lot of Bible study over the years. The teachings of Jesus are very clear. You cannot serve God *and* money — you have to choose.

Money and material possessions have addictive qualities. If you doubt that, all you have to do is look back to the 1929 stock market crash, which started the Depression. People were jumping out of windows on Wall Street. Those people were not thinking, "I'm not going to have any food to eat tonight. I might as well jump out of the window, because I'm going to starve to death." No, it wasn't that at all. They had enough money to survive on. They despaired because their lives were totally wrapped up with possessions. When so many of their possessions were suddenly gone, all of a sudden life had no further meaning.

Really and truly, it would be impossible for me to be a poor person as long as I have my health and my mind, because I am a highly educated person. I have degrees in economics and law. So I could become penniless, with absolutely nothing, and still work my way back up. Privilege and wealth are more than money. Living in the richest country in the world with so many opportunities and having a good mind and an excellent education, I didn't make myself poor. I simply got rid of my money.

Many people ask us questions, such as, "Have you provided for your children?" Well, I've got four children. Three of them have already graduated from college, and one is in college now. We've never suffered for anything. We don't live a Spartan life by any means, but we do live simply so that we can get by without having to devote large amounts of time to generating money.

Actually, I've never made more money in my life than I am making now — it just doesn't go in my personal pocket. In 1989, at Habitat for Humanity, we raised over $44 million in just one year. Forty-four million is far more money than I made in all my years in business. Of course, I'm not doing it alone, but I wasn't doing it alone when I was in business, either. You never do it all alone, never.

My goals and motivations have changed. Instead of business, I am just pursuing the common good. As Dr. Martin Luther King said, we all should work toward the establishment of the beloved community. Jesus taught us to pray, "Thy kingdom come, thy will be done on earth as it is in heaven." If you work for the coming of the beloved community, you have to be as concerned about your neighbors as you are about yourself. In order to generate income and services and housing and food and clothing for your neighbors, you must have as much fire in your belly as if you were doing it for yourself.

Unfortunately, many of the brightest minds are devoting all of their energies to making themselves richer. It's a sad commentary that at Harvard, our country's most prestigious educational institution, the business school is turning out financial analysts whose main desire is to make six-figure salaries within two years after they graduate. What a sick goal — to set out deliberately on a program to make grossly more money than they could use for their most extravagant needs!

We have one automobile in our family, even though it would be more convenient to have two or three. This is one way to establish limits. I walk a lot and I think I stay healthier because of it. It does cause little inconveniences: it takes longer to get from point A to point B, but I don't end up in the hospital. People who have all of these gidgets and gadgets, and two or three cars, and ride everywhere, and sit in plush chairs, and go home and sleep in a plush bed just end up sick in the hospital. A simpler lifestyle and eating simpler foods keeps you healthier, and you can go to bed at night with a clear conscience.

There is a point where it becomes sinful to consume and hoard so much, but I don't know exactly where that point is. I think it varies. One person, for example, may have more need for art, while another person may think art is just not important. God in His wisdom didn't make us the same. You can't set a rigid standard and say everybody must live exactly like this. Nonetheless, I do think moderation is called for in every aspect of our lives.

* * * * *

The advent of space travel meant that, for the first time, we got a God's-eye-view of the earth. You cannot see national boundaries from space — you just see it all laid out there. All boundaries in the world are artificially drawn, usually in blood. They are not God's lines at all. I think that if we see the earth as just one little fragile ball hanging in space, we will think differently about people who live on the other side of those artificial lines. We can't say we worked hard and we deserve what we've got, and those slobs over there didn't work hard so they should just die in squalor and misery, and it's no concern of ours.

A lot of the people who live in these poorer countries are poorer because we don't pay much for their coffee, or our country has restrictive trade policies, so they can't get much for their goods. We have tremendous advantages educationally, materially, and economically. We have the power to sit on their heads — and we do it. We also have the power to lift them up and help them and that is what we ought to do. We ought to see ourselves as fellow citizens of planet earth and be horrified when we, living in the lap of luxury, hear of fellow human beings who are suffering. The Bible is full of examples of how God judges those who are in the lap of luxury and don't do anything about those who are living in misery.

There are people who buy six TVs and they haven't got room for another one. Last year they bought three automobiles, went to the Caribbean, traveled all over to Europe and they are bored with all these trips where they lay around on the beach. They can't think of what to do with all of their money so they send a few crumbs to Habitat for Humanity. I'm not sure they get a blessing out of it. It's a help to us, but they're not going to get a blessing out of it, because it was not a sacrificial gift — it's a little piece of the leftovers.

At a conference on socially responsible investment in Atlanta, I challenged people to consider the option of giving their money away. Some people might keep the money, invest it wisely, and use it for social good, but I think there is a great temptation to take a giant share of it for yourself. It is so easy. You say, "By Golly, this is my money, so I'll decide. And I decide that I need a $100,000 per year salary."

I was on a radio program where they asked me about my salary. I said I make less than $12,000 a year from Habitat for Humanity. They asked, "Well, most heads of big multi-million dollar nonprofits draw $100,000 per year. Why aren't you doing that?" I said, "Because I have the power to do it doesn't mean I have the right to do it." We have committed ourselves to modest salaries so we can deliver the money where we say we will deliver it.

We need models of people who divest, so people will understand that it really is an option. A lot of people don't even consider that. They would rather say, "Well, no, I'll invest my money so it can be used for some socially redemptive purpose, but I'm going to keep my clutches on it, so that if anything goes bad I will always have a security blanket."

People with privilege ought to become familiar with movements that are doing significant things. Maybe they should invest their funds to get themselves elected to be a different kind of politician. But they have to be very careful to guard their motives and not get caught up on an ego trip. Jimmy Carter is a person who remained pretty committed to his ideals, both as President and since he left office. He has worked with us at Habitat for Humanity, and he is committed to human rights and sharing with the poor. I think he is a great example today of someone who is quite affluent — in terms of material wealth, position, power, influence, and prestige — who is using those resources for the larger good. We can all be part of helping to usher in the beloved community, a New Earth where righteousness prevails.

EDORAH FRAZER

Edorah, 29, teaches junior high school and does consulting for various schools. She has given $450,000 — 75% of her principal — to anti-racism, youth and environmental projects.

I was the youngest of seven children and grew up in Winnetka, Illinois, a wealthy suburb on the North Side of Chicago. During the Depression, my father's father agreed to help businesses get back into the black in return for a share of their stock. He was a brilliant accountant and the businesses he helped took off. So did his bank account.

My father never made much money on his own, but lived off the money he inherited from his father. He put a lot of it into his own business, but it was such a poor investment it was like pouring money down the drain.

I was raised and cared for by a Black woman named Gussie from the South Side of Chicago. She worked for my family from before I was born until I was in high school. I always noticed that her clothes were different and that she rode the bus while we drove. My first awareness of class differences came from her presence in our household.

Gussie would never sit in a chair, except in the kitchen. She always sat on the floor whenever we convinced her to come watch a TV show with us. I was annoyed by this and blamed it on my parents. But my mother pointed out that she always offered Gussie a chair — that it wasn't as though she forbade her to sit in a chair. It was very complicated, and I was angry about it. I also remember that my sister brought friends home and that my family didn't like them because they were of different class or ethnic backgrounds.

When I was in fifth grade, three of my grandparents died and there was a lot of talk in the family about their wills. Because my sister had married a Jewish man her share of the inheritance was reduced, while I was to receive some of her share because I was named after my uncle. It was very confusing: I had the right name and she married the wrong guy. I remember feeling that it was unjust.

When I was 16 my dad died, and I started receiving interest checks from the bank. It was only then that the fact that I would have money really came home to me, and I started asking how much I would ultimately receive. I discovered that at 25, each of us would receive over $500,000.

For many years, I argued with my mom and sisters about money and my feeling that I did not have a right to it. Why was it that the people down the block, or people on TV, or people across the ocean, didn't have it? It was stupid for me to have it. No one in my family could hear that; it was threatening to them. Although I'm sure that on some level they knew I was right, they never admitted any sympathy with my feelings. I was bashing my head against the wall, and being the youngest in the family didn't make it any easier. When we went on vacations or out to fancy meals I hated every minute of it. But I was one little voice in this huge family of consumers.

To them, money was not related to anyone else's life. But in my mind it was outrageous that I should have so much more money than over 90% of the rest of the world. It just seemed so simple and obvious, I felt an absolute conviction.

*   *   *   *   *

My most powerful exposure to social inequities came through my church work. When I was a teenager, my church had a youth minister from Georgia, named Rita. She was a nun who had done anti-poverty work in Appalachia, and who came to Winnetka determined to open some eyes. She sure succeeded with some of us kids!

I was getting sick of high school, so I arranged a work- study program where I worked with Rita three mornings a week for credit. One day she said, "Take me on a tour of Winnetka and tell me about it." She asked me questions like, "What do the women do after they take their children to school?" I said, "Well, they play tennis or bridge and they have women's clubs." Rita shook her head — she'd never heard of this. When I saw her shake her head, I shook mine too, not understanding her puzzlement. It was a bizarre meeting of cultures.

One day she said, "Let's go see Chicago." Well, kids in Winnetka did *not* go to Chicago — it was "too dangerous" or "dirty" — but I went with her anyway. She suggested that we get on the "El" — the elevated train — and ride to the end of the line. We sat there looking out the windows and rode all the way to the South Side of Chicago and back. I was amazed by what I saw. Then she said, "Let's go work in a soup kitchen in Chicago." So we did! In one morning, we'd ride to Chicago and back to Winnetka. The contrasts were staggering. Later, I worked for a hotline in Chicago and talked on the phone with people with the most unbelievable stories of child abuse and drugs. My mind was opened very wide and fast in just a few months.

Religion influenced me, especially during those years I was going into Chicago. I saw everything in terms of God and faith — including my privilege and the people I met. My faith fed my boiling sense of injustice, and all those years of indignation helped shape my decision to give my wealth away. Giving away wealth was a matter of religious conviction for me, although the priests and ministers around me weren't saying that. They had to keep their jobs in Winnetka — they couldn't possibly say anything like that in such a wealthy community.

Sometime during the year after I graduated from college, I went to the Dover Public Library in New Hampshire and, barely knowing what I was doing, asked the librarian about alternative investments and giving. She was mystified; no one had ever asked for such information. She looked up lots of entries in the *Reader's Guide*, and we were there for an hour bumping into each other looking at reference books. Finally, we found an article in *Fortune* and one in *Ms.* about alternative investments. The librarian really got into it; for weeks afterwards she kept sending me articles. I wrote down the name of every organization in those articles.

The next time I was in Boston, I visited one of those organizations, the Haymarket People's Fund. I said that I wanted the *Directory of Socially Responsible Investing*, and a staff member named Linda dug around in the closet and got it. I remember looking through it while Linda was getting me some other book — and I started laughing and crying! I just could not believe that other people in the world were doing this! And not just a few, but a lot of them! I realized how lucky I was to have stumbled upon this, coming from my background which had sheltered me from such ideas. Finally I would have someone to talk with!

I immediately ordered five copies of the *Directory* and sent them to all the people I knew who had money and an active social consciousness. Within a month I was doing talks at colleges to educate people about Haymarket. It was like a whirlwind! I had no activist background, and the whole political and alternative investment realm was completely new to me. It was a big romance!

In 1985, I went to a Haymarket conference hoping to resolve my feelings about giving all my money away. At the first workshop, we introduced ourselves and stated our goals for our money. I said my goal was to give it all away. The introductions stopped short. People freaked out. I was so surprised — I thought everyone there would have that goal!

Several middle-aged women in the group cautioned, "You have to think about the future!" One older woman who had been shaking her head as I spoke presented many different reasons why I shouldn't give it all away. One reason came from a liberal perspective: "Keep the money and you'll be able to fund things for the rest of your life."

Whenever I talked with people — at the conference, and other places, too — about the possibility of my giving my money away, people would question me: "Did I really want to do this? What if an emergency came up? What about when you have children? What if you get sick? What if you want to give in the future and you don't have any left to give?" I would answer, "I'll handle it in the way most people have to handle it. So it might be tough, but why should my life be so much easier than someone else's? Why should I have a margin of privilege over other people? I still keep tons of advantages that won't just disappear when I've given all the money away: I'm healthy, well- educated, and bright. I feel confident about always being able to get a job. As far as not being able to fund things in the future, that's not an issue for me. I don't like being a philanthropist. I don't like the mechanics of giving away money and I don't like having that power. I want to give the money and be finished with it, so I can spend my time and care on other things." [1]

A year later, at another Haymarket conference, we did an exercise to identify others with similar interests. I asked, "Who has seriously considered giving away all of their money?" and to my surprise and excitement ten people came forward. So we held a workshop about giving away assets, and four of us met afterwards to talk more.

It was so good talking together that the four of us met again after the conference, and later became an ongoing support group. The group provided me with political and practical information, both of which I needed. After my years of anger about injustice came several years of learning about giving and trying to develop some political strategy. I'm not much of a strategic thinker, and I'm not very political. I've had to learn about these things while maintaining my own sense of right and wrong and my own sense of justice. The group helped me move forward in my decision.

*　　　　*　　　　*　　　　*　　　　*

In September 1986, I turned 25 and received all my inherited money. Although I had been getting quarterly interest checks since my dad died, this was the first time I had access to the principal. I asked for it all to be sent to me from the Northern Trust Company in Chicago in its current form of stock certificates. I wanted to give the stock away directly, because I knew that if I sold it I would have to pay capital gains tax. I've been a war tax resister, so I wanted to avoid taxes, if possible. Not long after, $400,000 in stock certificates arrived in the mail.

I made charts about each stock. I was curious to see what heinous products I was helping to produce so I wrote down what each company produced, and I found out many interesting things — for instance, that the Morton Salt Company not only makes table salt, but the booster rockets for nuclear missiles.[1] What a weird association! According to my calculations, my stocks were worth about $423,000. I also had $150,000 in cash and government bonds, but since there were no tax liabilities with that money I decided to deal with it later.

I sat at the kitchen table and took out two thick folders I had collected, one full of grant proposals from different organizations and another full of tax information. Then I looked at the stock certificates, all very flowery looking with different colors and embossed stamps. They looked like money but bigger and each stated the number of shares I owned in that company. I spread them all out on the kitchen table and started making phone calls. I called Haymarket, I called an accountant and a variety of tax people to find out what I should do. It was mid-December, one of the last days in the year to sell stocks or give money away for the tax year. I thought, "I'm going to give it away anyway, so why have a huge tax liability? I might as well just get rid of this stuff now."

I decided to place all my stocks into a donor-advised fund I set up with The Funding Exchange, the progressive foundation network, of which Haymarket is a part. That way The Funding Exchange would hold on to all the money — I could never get it back — but they would distribute it with my advice, over whatever period of time made sense to me.

About two days before Christmas, I gathered up the stock certificates and went down to E.F. Hutton. They knew I was coming, so they had ready all the forms I would need in order to give the stocks to The Funding Exchange. People were walking by outside the window — it was Christmas season and we were just doing this little piddly paperwork that, for me, had huge significance. I was in a very good mood; we were laughing and eating Christmas candy. A man walked in and I said, "You know what, this is a major event in my life, and to you guys it's business as usual!" He looked down, saw the stack of stock certificates and said, "I don't know what you're doing, but it's not normal business here to have a stack of stock certificates like that on our desks."

I had to go out to get something notarized, some release form, and the notary asked me to repeat, "I swear that I am doing this of my free will." I laughed and said, "I swear." I went back to E.F. Hutton, finished the paperwork, and said, "thanks." It was finished in half an hour.

Outside, it was raining, and across the street I saw two Salvation Army men with a bucket ringing a bell. The rain was falling on me and I started to cry. It felt really clean, so simple. Although I was happy I thought, "I'm lonely. I wish I had done this with someone." Then immediately I thought, "No, it's good that I did it alone, because it is a very individual act. Ultimately, I am alone in this decision. It's my story."

I crossed the street, took out all the money in my wallet and put it into the Salvation Army bucket. Since it was raining no one was giving them money; everyone was rushing past. I put the money in the bucket and looked at the two and said, "You two are *gentlemen*!" They didn't know what was going on; the notary didn't know what was going on; no one knew what was up! But to me, everything was falling into place just as it should.

I found a pay phone and called Christopher and Chuck, from my support group. Christopher wasn't in so I left a message on his answering machine, "I DID IT! I DID IT!" I reached Chuck and we cheered on the phone.

Later, while driving home, someone cut me off, and I cursed at the driver. The world returns, but for about 20 minutes I had experienced something ethereal and magical.

*　　　　*　　　　*　　　　*　　　　*

For six months after my giving, I recorded every dollar I spent and found out that I was living on about $14,000 a year. That was the first time I knew how much it would take to support myself. I always worked, but earned less than half my expenditures, counting on unearned income to make up the difference.

One night as I was falling asleep, I found myself calculating how much money I used each year from my inheritance and how many years I would be able to live at my current lifestyle if I didn't give away any more. "Using $8,000 unearned income a year, in 15 years it will be gone!" And with a sense of panic, I woke up. Then I realized, "Oh, my God, that's totally irrational. I'm not going to be living like this for 15 years — I'm going to be earning my living starting next year as a teacher."

That made me realize how fearful I was about the end of the inherited money. Giving away $400,000 was comfortable. My last $100,000 is still large enough to make me feel that I don't have a right to it, but looking at giving it away is not easy or comfortable — I'm afraid. For the world, $400,000 is more important than $100,000, but for me the $100,000 will be the most important giving. Getting support from other people will be critical in times to come.

My biggest fears are about changing how I spend money in my daily life: setting limits, such as on how often I go out for breakfast or make long distance phone calls. It's just like dieting to me — when I start to count calories I want more. If I make a restriction, I want to break through it. Yet I don't want to feel cushioned by money any more. Having money feels like a film wrapped around me, a kind of numbing. While the good of struggling can be over-romanticized, I think there's something vital about concern for your bread and butter. If you never go into the kitchen and someone always brings you food, you're less involved with the stuff of life. The same is true if I never have to work or if I never have to clean my own house.

When I'm afraid I remind myself that I still have many sources of security — companionship, education, health, intelligence — these are very concrete advantages. I have a certain confidence coming largely from having had money. For instance, I feel I have the right to go into a lawyer's office to get assistance, or to go into a government office to complain about something. Ultimately, when I examine my feelings about security, it is religion and faith that sustain me the most.

Even though I talked so much about it through the years, about half my family knows I gave my money away and half doesn't know yet. When some of my sisters asked me, I simply said, "I gave most of it away." One of my sisters, the most materialistic, said, to my surprise, "You've been a long time coming to that decision. How do you feel about it?" I said, "I feel good; I think it was right." She added, "Great. If others in the family give you flack about it, I hope you'll let me help however I can." Coming from the person who is farthest from me politically, that felt especially supportive.

Outside my family, my best friends all know. It's been great for me to talk about my money. I would encourage anyone to "come out" about it. Every time I hear people say, "People will hurt you somehow if they know you have money," my feeling is, "Not as much as you're hurting yourself." It's worth it — no matter what — it's worth it to come out of that closet.

I would encourage people who care what their money represents to look deep inside, into that wise part of themselves. Listen to everyone, but then go off and lie down in a field and figure out what's right for you. I couldn't have come to my decision just by thinking about it — I had to travel by myself, observe people, and pay attention to the earth. I noticed my unhappiness with the imbalanced state of the world, and drew my conclusions — that I am part of that imbalance, but I can choose to shift the balance a little bit by my own actions.

1. Editor's note: Since this interview, Morton Salt has split off from the company which made booster rockets.

SALLIE BINGHAM

Sallie, 53, has authored a novel, short stories, various articles, and recently, her memoirs. She founded and serves as director of the Kentucky Foundation for Women and is an outspoken advocate for women's rights.

I grew up outside of Louisville, Kentucky, in one of those suburbs that can be found all over the world: big houses and long driveways, beautiful grass, trees and gardens. I grew up with two older brothers and a younger brother and sister. The family business included a statewide monopoly newspaper, a television station, several radio stations and a printing plant. It was a big industry for a small, poor state and packed enormous political and economic power.

The boys were expected to go to work in the family business, and the two oldest were aimed in that direction. It was not really clear what the rest of us were going to do. We were operating on the English model where the oldest sons take over and the younger ones either go abroad, go into the ministry or become soldiers. As a girl, the expectation was that I would get married and that would take care of me. Since I loved writing, it was assumed that I would continue — but as a hobby, rather than as a profession.

I grew up around condescending attitudes — towards women, towards people who don't have money, towards people who are disadvantaged, and towards people who were Black. People were constantly measured by lots of unspoken criteria. As a child, I sensed that we were special for some reason, but the reason remained mysterious because money was never discussed. We were just different from other people.

Nobody ever talked about money, ever, so there was no way to know how much money we had or how we would inherit it. That was all a mystery until I was in my early twenties. In fact — and it must seem strange, but I've heard other people say this too — I was quite convinced that we really didn't have very much, in spite of our spectacular way of living, because there was so much anxiety about money.

My parents' anxiety was expressed in their fear of display. Don't wear something that looks expensive, whether it's a fur coat or jewels. Don't drive an expensive car — drive a small, American car. Don't be lavish with presents to friends. Be careful about what you spend money on. As children, we had very little pocket money, which I think is typical of a certain kind of wealthy family, and we used to scrimp and save to buy Christmas presents in the ten-cent store.

Of course when you consider the price of the house, or the fact that there were five servants living in it, then you realize the great contradictions. As a child, however, those expenses were taken for granted — they seemed beyond money, just the way life was. It was a long time before I even realized, for instance, that the servants were paid. I thought they were just there. When I found out what the house and servants meant about our wealth, I felt a sense of shame — that the family had made the mistake of spending money in a conspicuous way. These contradictions were very confusing.

As in a great many upper-class families, I was largely raised by servants. I identified more with the Black servants and with my nurse than I did with the adult family members, the people who were running that world. I gradually recognized the difference between my family and those servants. One clue was the servants' lack of mobility. Because they didn't have cars, they couldn't leave the house unless somebody could be found to drive them, so they didn't go places. Eventually, I realized that was because they had so little money and I felt sorry for them. My mother felt it was condescending of me to express sympathy for them, and so I felt quite guilty about that. I didn't feel condescending — I just felt sorry for them. I also was aware that the servants worked terribly hard — they got out and dug in the dirt and cut grass and washed floors. When I realized that all their work did not produce very much money for them, I felt sorry.

In high school I first became aware that I had more money than a lot of other people. This was at a small private girls' school in Louisville, where everybody was comfortably off. But finally one young woman arrived on a scholarship. The first time I went to visit her I was amazed to hear that her parents were divorced, which was unheard of at that time. She lived in a little, rather grim, run-down apartment in the city, not out in the suburbs. I was almost embarrassed for her, thinking, "Nobody should have to live this way, and if you do, your friends shouldn't have to see it." I realized then that I lived a very protected life.

Ours was a very verbal family, fast on the repartee. If you made the mistake of not completing your sentence or using a split infinitive you would be demolished. It seemed dangerous to say much of anything unless you were certain that what you were going to say was very funny and very caustic, the kind of grown- up wit most children don't command. Because my family was so competitive, nobody dared to show any feelings for fear of being ridiculed, so I didn't really know if anyone shared my feelings.

My family strongly valued giving money, although in very traditional ways. If a charity was having a fundraising drive they were obliged to make a handsome contribution. But they gave money only to conventional charities. They were supposed to be available when their friends were soliciting for their charities, but they were not supposed to give anything that would interfere with their lifestyles. That would have been really strange! Nobody listened to what Jesus said. We went to church all the time, but didn't hear the words.

A lot of denial came from not wanting to acknowledge how the money came into the family. Our money came from Standard Oil, which I didn't know for many years. I knew even less about Standard Oil's role in the Second World War. A lot of the big American corporations had ties with Germany before the war, and continued to do substantial amounts of trade with Germany during the war. The U.S. Government even supported it. Standard Oil was actually fueling the German war machine! I almost died when I found out!

The money which allowed my grandfather to buy the newspaper companies came to him through the widow of one of the original Standard Oil partners, Henry Flagler. Mrs. Flagler married my grandfather and she died eight months later under very mysterious circumstances. A huge scandal and much litigation followed, but it never came to anything. To this day, nobody really knows what happened to her, but many people feel, I think with some validity, that she was murdered. It was horrible, because whatever happened to her, she was victimized and her money had certainly had something to do with it. (Of course, this whole story was concealed — I only found out as an adult. I didn't even know she existed when I was a child.)

Old liberal families like mine believe in the American Dream, believe that anybody in America can get to be president, believe that this is an equal society, and believe that racism no longer happens. But when they look with any introspection at their own lives, they have to realize that the money did not come through working our way up through the system — it came through a windfall, some good luck, and was then used to make more money. If they really looked they would see it's extremely hard to get rich in this country, as it is anywhere.

*   *   *   *   *

I knew from very early on that I was treated differently from the men in the family. Sometimes these were very nice ways — for instance, I didn't have to break my back trying to run the family business. But it also meant condescension, lack of appreciation for my intelligence and my character. It also meant a willingness to use me as a pawn in their power games, and to push me around as was convenient. A lot of women in my position have had that experience. These men also love us to some degree, but in tight power situations what counts is their belief that women can be pushed around.

I was on the boards of the family-held companies. At one point all the women were thrown off the boards, but I refused to resign. This made them angry, because they wanted us to go discreetly. When they asked me to resign I asked them why. They couldn't explain it to me, so I said, "I'm not going to resign without even knowing why. I'm not incompetent, so I'm not going to accept that as an explanation." They didn't want anybody on the board who was going to ask questions. As it happened, I was one of the few who did ask questions. Questions like, "Why did we lose $1 million on cellular radio?" Even very responsible financial kinds of questions — they just didn't want to hear them. They never had heard them before, and they didn't want to hear them now.

Finally, through all kinds of misunderstandings and manipulations and because I owned only a small amount of stock, they succeeded in forcing me off. All of that brought some public attention, which they had hoped to avoid. I was blamed for letting other people see what was really going on. Of course, that was one thing I felt had to happen and should happen with big corporations. People should know the way they're being operated. When there is a crisis, there's a lot of turmoil and anger and people tend to scapegoat somebody, instead of examining and changing the system.

I decided that I would sell my share and I offered it to the family. But they wouldn't meet what I felt was a fair price, even after I had come down about $10 million. Meanwhile, father, for his own reasons, decided to sell the company.

Many women have gotten less than their share of the family money, and that would have happened to me, too, the way it had been set up. Some women don't find out until the will is read, until it is too late to do anything about it. I was fortunate to find out sooner, because the sale of the family companies inevitably meant that the finances were laid bare. For the next couple of years of protracted negotiations, I got a lot of good legal and financial advice, and I ended up getting a share equal to that of my siblings.

My early training taught me that if you're rich you owe something to the world, but I was never very interested in conventional charities. I have never been convinced that they change the status quo — in fact I think they support the status quo. I wanted to give a substantial amount of money for women, because all my life I've been aware that women often have a harder time than men. And, since I'm a writer, I wanted to do something for writers and artists, who generally have a difficult time surviving financially. So I set up the Kentucky Foundation for Women, which supports individual artists and writers.

I put $10 million into the Foundation. I knew that the proceeds from the sale of my portion of the family companies would be $60 million. Out of that, about $30 million is still tied up in trusts and about $10 million went to fees and taxes — there was just no way around that. So the $10 million is about a half of what I received.

The Foundation gives away about $250,000 a year. We also publish a quarterly called *The American Voice*, and run a house in the country that's used by women's groups for retreats. Our goal is to support art that successfully treats social concerns, and to support women artists who would never make it otherwise in the narrowly competitive art world.

I enjoy reading letters from people we have helped through the Foundation. I remember one from a young woman in southern Indiana who has become a puppet maker. We sent her to study with the Bread and Puppet Theater in Vermont. She came back and made her first two puppets, life-sized figures of old women, each of them with a complete life story. She manipulates them so that you forget that they aren't real, and goes around to people locked in old-age homes and communicates with them through her stories.

This Foundation isn't supporting the "arts" as some pleasant thing that you go to and sit half-asleep all evening. It's social change, through helping women succeed in the arts, and working against the stereotyping of women. The arts themselves challenge the stereotypes: through visual images, words and music, we bring about constructive change. I've been pleased that we made the mission of the Foundation clearly for social change.

JOE COLLINS

Joe is the co-founder of the Institute for Food and Development Policy, where he has worked as a researcher and author since 1975. The Institute is dedicated to educating the public on global food and hunger issues.

I was born at the end of World War II. My mother and father met when my father was 74 and my mother was 43, so my growing up was a little unusual. By the time I was born my parents felt they might not be around much longer, so they wanted to teach me what they knew while I was still young.

My parents had independently made a sizeable amount of money — not one of the great industrial fortunes of America, but a couple of million bucks each, in those day's dollars. They thought I should learn the value of money and exactly how investments work — real estate, the stock market, bonds, and so forth. I was an unusual child in that I was familiar with all the security market jargon by the time I was in early grade school. In order to teach me the value of money, my parents required me to get jobs, so I worked as a caddie at the country club and delivered newspapers. When I was 12, I bought Pepsi-Cola stock with my earnings.

Since both my parents retired when I was born, they didn't just teach me during weekends, but perpetually! When I came home from school and said that we studied this or that in American history, my father would often say that he recalled it differently from the way that I was being taught. Since my father had lived through a good part of what we call American history, he was a more credible authority than my 28-year-old teacher. He never said, "Don't believe what's in the book." He just kept telling me stories and his ideas. From very early on, I learned that what was printed in the book might not be the way it really was in the world, and that there are other views of reality than the authoritative ones.

My parents set up a trust fund with pay-out periods at different points in my life, to be completely paid out when I reached age 26. My father died when I was 13, and my mother wrote the bank's trust department saying if she died I did not need a guardian — I was able to be on my own. She died a year later. In the state of Ohio a guardian was not required at the age of 14; it was up to the court. In my case, the probate court judge had never dealt with such a situation before, but he was willing to give it a try.

I lived in the family home, and my parents' cook still came to cook for me, along with a Black man who came a couple of days a week to clean the house. However, neither were authority figures, so I was on my own from the age of 14. I went to a day school operated by the Jesuits in Cincinnati, Ohio, and concentrated on being a good student, and I did not do anything that made the trust department, the police or the courts want to rein me in.

I delivered newspapers and my route included an organization of Catholic priests, the Maryknoll Fathers, who worked mainly in the Third World. From time to time, I talked to this or that priest who had spent a good part of his life in a Third World country — one priest in South America, another in China. My parents had said that travelling broadened one's life, and there I was with a lot of money and freedom, so the summer after my mother died I went to Chile.

I stayed in a school in a relatively poor neighborhood of Santiago. While my main activity was learning Spanish, what I was really doing was seeing incredible poverty for the first time. There had been a major earthquake, and there were still quite a few displaced people who had already been poor but were now even worse off. I learned most of my initial Spanish talking to beggars asking me for food.

I continued to go to a different Maryknoll mission every summer. I lived in the Altiplano in Peru. I stayed with the Mayan people in the mountains in Guatemala. I visited Mindinao in the Philippines. The people I met were quite outspoken about the impact of the United States on their countries. After five years I began to question a lot that was being done in the name of the United States — what the U.S. government and U.S.-based corporations were doing in those countries. I began to think that rather than spend my life going to the Third World to help the poor, I should find a way to help change the impact of the United States in the world.

For instance, while in Chile, I learned that two big copper companies had a tremendous effect on the whole national economy, yet the lion's share of the profits was taken out of the country to the U.S. The people in Chile knew all about this, but people in the U.S. did not. I thought maybe I could inform people in the U.S. about it.

After I graduated from a Jesuit high school I studied to be a Maryknoll priest, thinking that I would educate fellow Catholics and non-Catholic Americans about what was being done in our name overseas. However, I became increasingly uncomfortable with representing the Catholic Church and eventually decided to leave Maryknoll. I took with me a resolve to spend my life "missionizing" in the U.S., the country of my birth, to help to change its ways, to convert it, to gain self-understanding. There were clearly more than enough Chileans to work in Chile, Mexicans in Mexico, and Filipinos in the Philippines. I learned a lot about myself working overseas, including the fact that I have the responsibility to work in my own country and probably can do my best work here.

So, after six years in Maryknoll, I left and went to Columbia University and Union Theological Seminary. It was the height of the anti-Vietnam War movement, and I soon got involved. The experiences I had gained in Third World countries enabled me to understand the Vietnam War. I saw it was yet another effort to impose the control of an imperialist country on people who were simply trying to control their own lives. The U.S. propaganda machine cast the war as a huge ideological struggle between "democracy" and "totalitarianism," but the ordinary Vietnamese were not thinking about ideology — they simply wanted to have some control over their beloved country, rice paddy and family.

Trying to stop the war shattered some of the myths I still held about American society. On one occasion I led a group of 200 people who ended up in prison for anti-war actions. We were just about the only white people in a prison that was built for 1,500, but held 3,000. Most of the people there were just waiting for trial because they couldn't afford bail, and some had been there for a couple of years. Of course, we got out after a couple of weeks because we had the means. But spending those couple of weeks in a federal detention center gave me a powerful sense of just how crude some of the mechanisms of this society are.

Because I had discovered the nature of the U.S. role abroad relatively early, I was in a position to lead many others into direct involvement with the movement. I also had the opportunity to know extraordinary people who were taking risks, such as Dan Berrigan and other Catholic anti-war people. I have known no period comparable to the late sixties. So much was going on, so much excitement, so many interesting people — I was happy to be part of that.

At the start of the war I was 21, and beginning to get payments of principal from the trust. I began to have problems with the idea of having money. So many needs cried out — how could I sit with money invested and not respond to those needs? Could I tell people, "I can help here, but I can't help there" or "Well, I've already given all I want to give this year"? I just couldn't do that.

I decided on my 22nd birthday that, over the following four years, I would give away everything I inherited. Two sets of factors were influencing me: first, what I would call objective needs; second, my own subjective needs.

I had not far to look to see objective needs: I knew of many people and projects that really needed money. For instance, the family of a classmate had a lot of financial problems — they were low-income working people to begin with, then the father had health setbacks, winter was coming in New Hampshire, and they were living in an uninsulated summer house with eight children.

How could I not help them get adequate shelter? I had the money. Sure, I thought, other people need houses, but I can't let that become my rationale for not helping one particular family. So without ever meeting them, I bought the family a house. Some people respond to needs by feeling, "Well, how can I help this person and not help the others?" The way I saw it, I could help this person, and then, if I wished, work on behalf of the others too.

Another objective need was the Vietnam War. I was outraged by the horrors perpetrated in the war, and felt we had to do everything possible to stop it. I put quite a bit of my money into funding films, some of which had an enormous impact on young people in the anti-war movement.

The subjective needs motivating me to give had to do with my feelings and relationship to the money. People who say, "I'm not going to give out all this money now, because I want it available to fund good things over time," are talking about being philanthropists. Philanthropists think about how to maintain the capital and even increase it, because after all, if they're going to use it, then the more the better, right? So then they spend a lot of energy constantly thinking about money. It wasn't that I didn't like handling money, it was that I liked it too much — it could be all-absorbing.

I could easily get into thinking, "Oh, I wish I had bought that stock" or "What money would I have made if I had done this?" I just didn't want to do that with my life.

Also, I didn't want to be seen as a source of money anymore. It makes no difference whether it's a million or a billion dollars — people will relate to those with money in terms of that money. I wanted to be known for myself and for my own deeds, not for my money.

My subjective and objective motivations coincided. I didn't want to be known for having the money, I didn't want to be thinking about making and giving money, and I felt moved to use money on efforts that needed the money right then. With those combined incentives, it didn't take me long to get rid of it. And I've had no regrets. There were so many more opportunities to give money away than I had money, $2 million didn't seem like much, even though it was worth about three times what it would be worth today.

While I felt good about funding films to mobilize people against the war, where I felt the most impact from my giving was through the more personal contributions. For example, in the situation I mentioned earlier about buying a house for a classmate's family, my friend told me years later that his father had been profoundly transformed by the gift. His wife, children and friends experienced him as a much nicer person. He just couldn't fathom that somebody whom he didn't know, just out of the blue, took care of this problem and bought them a house! His son told me that the gift brought a spiritual effect much more profound than just providing an adequate roof over their heads.

So I feel good about that and a few other instances like it. However, if I have had any effect at all in the world, it has been from being part of a continuing process which started long before I was born and which will go on long after I die. My contribution won't have been through the money I got from my parents, but through my work and my life.

I still meet people held back by having money. They have a hard time figuring out what to do with their lives. I know a couple of wonderful people who are also very generous with their money, but painfully stuck in trying to find their niche. The best use I made of some of my money was spending all those summers working as a volunteer in Third World situations. That infused my life with a clear sense of what I wanted to do.

In 1975, I met Frances Moore Lappé. It was at the University of Michigan, where we were both speakers. We were having lunch together, and I told her about the book I was working on that later become *Food First*. She exclaimed, "God, this is what I'd really like to be doing too!" She and I quickly decided that we would work together, and not just write a book about food and hunger but also provide an ongoing source of such information. So we founded the Institute for Food and Development Policy and that's what we have been doing ever since. We get to work with a lot of good people, at the Institute and around the world. I'm going to be doing this for the rest of my life; I have no desire to do anything else.

The only time I worry about not having the money is thinking about growing old. My grandmother lived to be 104 and my father lived to be 90. Because I'm not married and I don't have children, I sometimes wonder how I'll do when I get to be older. Now and then I visit cultures (like the Philippines) where people just adopt you. I imagine going there and being adopted by some peasant family who would take care of me!

I have described my reasons for giving away the money I inherited from my parents. But I wouldn't say that other people should try to make my reasons operate for them. People have to think it through for themselves. Anybody who is thinking at all along these lines is probably someone who does a lot of thinking anyway. I trust they'll find their own way.

GIVING IT AWAY

When people say to me, "Why should you give this much?" I say to them, "The way I see it, the question is: Why should I keep this much?!" We shouldn't put the burden of reasoning on the giving any more than the keeping.

— Carol Bernstein-Ferry

"Give away your wealth? Are you crazy? What about your security — you could get cancer or become disabled or get sued or who knows what in this insecure world! Have you thought about your children, the opportunities they'll miss for good education, travel, vacations? Won't you miss the power and freedom and peace of mind money gives you? Besides, your family has said for generations 'Don't touch the principal!' They'll disown you if you give it away!"

For those of us who gave away significant portions of our wealth, this is just a sampling of the injunctions and fears that swirled around us (from our friends and relatives, or within our own minds) before we took action. How did we get beyond these obstacles to the point of actually giving away substantial sums of money?

For most of us, the decision to give away our assets began with deeply-rooted motivations and influences which have proved far stronger than the buzz of concerns in our hearts, heads, and ears. While each of us has a unique story to tell, clear themes emerge in looking over our stories:

First, as children we were instilled with certain life-defining values by our families: belief in human equality...fairness...responsibility towards the community. Many of us absorbed these values from our parents and grandparents. Even though these same people may now be horrified by our interpretation of those principles, our family members were the source of those first important ethical lessons.

Second, most of us have been profoundly affected while growing up by experiences that brought us face-to-face with injustice. It might have been a trip through a poverty-stricken neighborhood of our home city, or some painful years as the class scapegoat, or a semester spent working with desperately poor people in the Third World. For whatever fluke of personality or environment, we did not try to shield ourselves from the pain of these experiences as most people do; instead, we brought the pain deep inside us where it coalesced into a resolve to fight injustice.

Spiritual beliefs also have played an important role for many of us. Whatever our religious backgrounds, the spiritual teachings we learned growing up often emphasized the oneness of humanity and the importance of a life based in service. Many of us were fortunate to encounter role models and opportunities that allowed us to put these teachings into practice.

As we grew into adults, these basic values were strengthened by political understandings. While some wealthy people seem to believe their money is a natural reward for risk-taking, hard work and genius (of themselves or their ancestors) many of us came to see that our wealth was built through a system that uses the labor of many (whose families do not inherit the resulting wealth) to inordinately benefit a few. Thus we began to feel more and more that the money was not rightfully ours, but belonged instead to the wider community. (One person who eventually gave all his inheritance to social change expressed it this way: "It felt to me like the moral equivalent of finding a wallet on the street and giving it back to its rightful owner.")

As this political awareness grew, many of us felt increasingly pained by the contradiction between the reality of poverty and the sums of money at our command. Giving away portions of our income didn't change the situation, since even when we were giving more than our peers were, our invested assets often just kept growing.

Even after our motivations for giving principal became strong, we still needed to deal with the practical questions raised by our worried friends and families. Some of us dealt with security concerns by buying disability insurance, establishing IRA accounts, and planning long-term budgets; some by keeping a substantial cushion of assets; others by choosing a very simple lifestyle and building a supportive community. We thought about our children by researching the costs of public universities, and by talking with friends who successfully raised families without much money. Some of us decided to give away assets slowly over months and years, so we could carefully assess the costs and benefits as we went along. Many of us had long honest talks with our families to minimize their estrangement. However we dealt with the practical issues, in the end giving away our wealth came down to a matter of faith. Most people we know, looking at the enormity of human problems, have little faith in change, and they feel their own contributions (whether $2 million or $25) as a pitiful drop in the bucket. They wonder, since that money can do a lot for their own lives and so little for the world, why bother? But somehow, most of us givers have come to a different conclusion: we believe our money makes a difference. In part, this belief stems from experiences many of us had as community activists, where we saw what a difference even small amounts of money could make. Many of us had the opportunity through the 60s and 70s to experience the power social change movements can have in changing people's lives. We had evidence that our money would matter.

Beyond all evidence, it has come down to faith — faith that change happens, that individual acts matter, that giving helps our lives feel more whole, and that we can trust our inner calling more than the worries that hold us back. We've taken the leap.

*   *   *   *   *

Deciding whether to give away substantial amounts of money can take considerable thought. If you are contemplating giving away a portion of your wealth, here are some questions to ask yourself:

How clear are you about your motivations? We encourage you not to act out of guilt, urgency or self-hatred, but to seek a clear strong sense of yourself and your values. Find other people to talk with who support your values.

How much money do you want to keep, and why? You might map out what you currently live on, and what you imagine for your future expenses. There are many fulfilling ways to live — what kind of lifestyle do you want? Do you know people who model different options? You can plan for realistic contingencies, without limiting your life by trying to anticipate every possible fearful event.

Will you make decisions independently, or in collaboration with others? Many people involve their partners, friends or families fully in their decision-making. Others seek input but make the final decisions themselves, and some go the whole route alone. We encourage you not to be isolated out of fear, and at a minimum, to talk over your thinking with a few people you trust.

Where do you want to have an impact? Are you drawn to specific issues — peace? the environment? social justice? Might you help exciting socially responsible businesses get off the ground, or help build local economies? Do you know where to find projects that inspire you, and how to evaluate them? Do you know how to get information about projects that traditionally do not have much access to funding — especially those of low-income people, women and people of color? Do you want a personal connection with the projects you help fund?

Over what period of time will you give? Some decide to give graduated amounts over a period of years, so they can assess how it feels as they go along. Others choose to give large amounts at once. Some are influenced by knowing they will inherit more at a future date. You can plan your giving in a way that best suits your internal and external needs.

What will be the mechanics of your giving? You could set up your own charitable structure, or give to an existing foundation, or give to specific groups or individuals. You may want to check the tax implications for different methods and timings. Will you give securities or cash? Anonymously or openly?

*   *   *   *   *

There are no right and wrong ways to give. Most of us floundered along, uncovering new questions as we went; we offer this list to you hoping it may ease your way.

However you give, you will probably find that the questions of how to take care of yourself and your loved ones and how to contribute to the world will continue. They have for us —and we work them out as we go along.

> There is one more thing I would say: just do it! We've often heard "keep your options open, be cautious." Well, there is enough of that! Don't be faint of heart. Go for it!

— Leslie Brockelbank

WHAT'S MY FAIR SHARE?

"somehow I get the feeling that the meek are
not going to inherit the earth in our lifetime"

When I give food to the poor, they call me a saint. When I ask why the poor have
no food, they call me a communist.

— Dom Helder Camara, Brazilian Archbishop [1]

"How can I determine my fair share in this unfair world?" Almost all of us whose
stories are told here grappled with this question, each in our own way. To answer it,
we had to look beyond our immediate families and neighborhoods — to our towns or
cities, our country, and the world — and make some sense of the injustices we saw.

First we needed a sense of perspective. Sure we're well-off, but how well-off? Most
of us (and this is true for people of any class background) live in neighborhoods
surrounded by people similar to us, so it's easy to feel "ordinary" no matter what our
situation. For the wealthy, this sense of sameness is reinforced by TV and magazines
and movies, where rich people abound and almost everyone seems comfortably
affluent. Most Americans like to think of themselves as middle-class, but life for a
"middle class" family living on $118,000 a year is significantly different from life for
another "middle-class" family living on $18,000 a year. [2]

The charts that follow offer a view of the spectrum of wealth in the U.S.

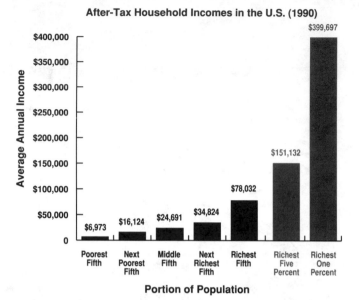

The above Congressional Budget Office projections were based on data from 1980 through 1988.[3]

Wealth is the monetary value (adjusted for debts) of what households own — consumer durables (houses, cars, stereos, etc.) plus financial assets (stocks, bonds, savings accounts, property, life insurance policies, etc.).[4]

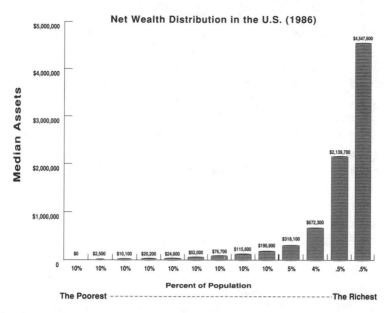

Net Wealth Distribution in the U.S. (1986)

In the above chart the population is organized from poorest to richest in groups of 10% (until the final 10% when the chart is divided into smaller percentages). Thus, the bar graph in the first 10% represents the net worth of the poorest 10% of the population (and so on). The median indicates that equal numbers of people have more as have less within that subgroup.

The average *net worth per subgroup is different than the median in that a handful of people who have a lot more or a lot less can pull the average in one direction or the other. If this chart were of the average net wealth distribution, the most striking differences would be that the poorest 10% would have a **negative** net worth (-$1,700) and the richest half of one percent of the population would have 50% more (+ $6,839,900).* [5]

Looking at these figures gives us a more accurate sense of where we stand. More than half the population have an after-tax *household* income (not individual income) of less than $25,000. Coincidentally, more than half the adults in the U.S. own assets of less than $25,000. Even if our assets are "only" $500,000, we have more than 95% of other Americans. In fact, the top 1% of the population controls almost one-third of the total wealth in the country, while half the population owns only 4.3% of the total wealth.

This being the case, some of us could see that even if we don't *feel* unusually well-off, we are very rich indeed — in income, net assets, or both — on a national scale. Once we understood these disparities, the next logical question was, "Well, *why* do I have so much more than others?" A common myth in America (on which many of us were raised) is that anyone who really tries can make it. Are those people on the low end of the charts just less smart and hardworking than our families? Were our grandparents (or whoever made our fortunes) bold leaders who were rightly rewarded for their ingenuity and risk-taking?

To answer why there are rich and poor in the U.S. — or more precisely, why a small percentage of us have fantastically more wealth than the vast majority — takes sorting through a maze of factors about capitalism: the way money makes money; the way many people's labor is turned into a few people's capital; the way our tax structure benefits the wealthy; the effects of racism and sexism; the impact of the huge military budget on social spending; and so on. Eventually those of us who gave principal sorted out our personal understandings of these issues and resolved that the differences between the rich and poor in this country were *not* justifiable — nor inevitable, nor tolerable. Perhaps our grandfathers who started factories *were* brilliant and bold, but they still didn't deserve to end up with 100,000 times more money than their employees. And when our $500,000 in stocks brings us a return of $50,000 a year without our lifting a finger, while millions of hardworking families work a whole year to earn far less (often finding themselves deeper in debt) — that's not fairness, that's a painfully skewed economic system.

Having compared ourselves with others in this country, where do we fit relative to the rest of the people in the world, where the average per person income is $800 per year? Not surprisingly, the picture of injustice is even starker when viewed globally: [6]

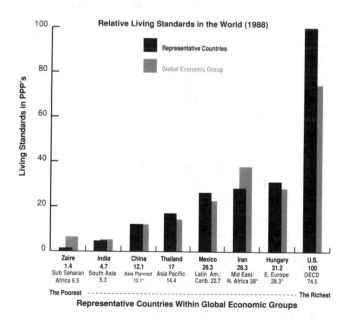

Purchasing Power Parity (PPP) ratios are units used by the United Nations to estimate the relative cost of living for people in different countries.

The economic groups are based on the income classification system usedby the World Bank to aid comparisons among countries at a similar stage of development. 7

The Organization for Economic Cooperation and Development (OECD) comprises the world's developed industrial nations. Twenty-one of OECD's 24 member countries are in the World Bank's "high-income group."

The representative countries we selected (one per economic group) had PPP ratios which corresponded fairly closely with the average PPP ratios of their economic group. However, we made two exceptions — the U.S. is at the richest end of the scale, and Zaire is at the poorest.

We can see from this chart that even the *average* American household in 1990, with an after-tax income of about $25,000 a year, lives on vastly more than most of the world. Again, we asked ourselves why such a big gap exists between rich and poor. Could the poorer countries eventually "pull themselves up by their bootstraps," become more developed, and then enjoy the U.S.'s level of material prosperity? No, we determined, the "developing" world could never become as materially rich as the U.S., since the U.S. and other wealthy nations already consume a very large (and growing) share of the earth's non-renewable resources. [8]

As The Worldwatch Institute put it in their *State of the World 1991*:

> Long before all the world's people could achieve the American dream the planet would be laid waste...Those in the wealthiest fifth of humanity have...pumped out two thirds of the greenhouse gases that threaten the earth's climate...and release almost 90% of the chlorofluorocarbons that destroy the earth's protective ozone layer. Clearly, even 1 billion profligate consumers is too much for the earth. [9]

But why do the industrialized countries have so much more than their fair share? Again, a complex web of factors confronted us — the history of colonization and imperialism, wealthy landowners growing "cash crops" like coffee for export instead of food for people locally, the brutal repression of people struggling for better conditions, the enormous burden of Third World debt to the First World, the role of the military in enforcing economic arrangements, etc. — but we ultimately came to similar conclusions after sorting it all out: Analogous to how the wealthiest in this country continue to receive the lion's share of the wealth at the expense of the working class and poor, the U.S. and industrialized countries accumulate much of their wealth at the expense of Third World countries. The wealthy of the world have more control over how economic and political decisions get made, and are more than willing to use that control to further their own advantage.

Witness the way multinational corporations extract raw materials and food from poorer countries (ores, cotton, coffee, fruit, etc.) and shift factories to places where the wages are lowest or the environmental restrictions the most lax. This control allows them to purchase at low prices, process at low labor costs, and sell for hefty profits.

> Look at the tags...inside your shirts, on the back of your cassette recorders. Most of us...would never be able to afford these commodities if it were not for the grossly

underpaid labor of women of color around the world who slave to produce them....Cheap labor is never cheap for the person who performs it. It is made cheap for the benefit of those who consume the products of that labor. South African coal is the cheapest coal in the world because Black coal miners slave and die in South African coal pits for less than 30 cents a day.

— Audré Lorde [10]

Once we concluded just how unfair so many giant economic institutions of the world really are, we struggled with what to do. While thus far humans beings seem not to have realized *any* economic system that, in practice, is both prosperous and just: we believed that we must continue to seek one.

Mahatma Gandhi, the revered leader of the independence movement in India, was also a brilliant ethical thinker who dedicated his life to creating a world where all people would be provided a rightful share. In his writings, he spelled out these guidelines of ideal economic, ecological and social fairness: [11]

- Nature produces enough to support our needs, but not more. If we take more than we need we may be borrowing from future generations or hurting nature.

- People have a right to an honorable livelihood and to having their basic needs met. Basic needs include a balanced diet, decent housing and health care, the education of children, and the search for spiritual self-realization.

- All other wealth beyond that belongs to the community. The community may grant more to individuals if it believes doing so benefits the general welfare, but such wealth is a privilege, not a right, and may not be allowed to injure the community.

Gandhi was not altogether optimistic that society would accept these principles peacefully:

...so long as the wide gulf between the rich and the hungry millions persists....a violent and bloody revolution is a certainty one day unless there is a voluntary abdication of riches and the power that riches give, and a sharing of them for the common good. [12]

A successor of Gandhi named Vinoba Bhave succeeded in putting the "voluntary abdication of riches" into practice — to some degree. He convinced wealthy landowners in India to give some of their land holdings to the landless poor. Over the years, the land gift or "Bhoodan" movement received hundreds of thousands of acres. Then "Gramdan" villages, which were cooperatively owned and managed by the villagers, were organized on the land.

Those of us whose stories are recounted in this book also wished to "voluntarily abdicate" some of our wealth back to the community. But how much? If Gandhi's ideal world were in place now, our fair share would be clear. But since we're not living in an equitable system, we each needed to work out some practical standards for determining our fair share in the present world, even as we work to change it. A few of us came up with precise standards, such as sociologist Charles Gray who figured out and lived on the "World Equity Budget." Most of us, though, after listening to our hearts, developed a few general principals, and are still struggling to this day with the compromises.

* * * * *

In searching for how to determine your fair share — which affects how much money to keep and how much to give away — here is a list of issues to think about. Each of us came to terms with these issues in different ways:

Is it fair to live off investment income? Chuck Collins felt that receiving investment income was like finding a wallet on the street that wasn't his — the honest thing to do was give it back. John Steiner, on the other hand, felt that using his resources to fund his own work, work that contributed greatly to the world, was a valuable use of the money. Tracy Gary felt fine about using investment income to cover her basic living expenses, but wanted to earn by her own efforts whatever she needed for travel and other luxuries. What's your viewpoint? Does it feel right to live on unearned money? Why or why not? Do you do a greater good by refusing to benefit from an unfair system, or by using your privileges to support your work for a better world?

What standard of living feels right? Tracy Gary wanted to feel nurtured by her surroundings — not by living at a sumptuous level of luxury, but by having enough "extras" that she felt renewed for her work in the world. Charles Gray had a very different standard. He agreed everyone needs treats, but for him sharing one ice cream cone with a friend was sufficient — he didn't need a whole meal. He believed having a special experience was very much in one's attitude. What nurtures you? How do you determine what level of luxury feels right? To whom do you compare yourself?

When do you buy private solutions to unmet social needs? In this society, many things that should be available to everyone — quality education and health care, streets that are safe and clean, secure and spacious housing, clean air and water and access to natural beauty — are, instead, expensive privileges. How do you feel about buying these, when others should have them but don't? Edorah Frazer didn't want to buy lots of special privileges; she believed that having to deal with the same difficulties most people face made her more real, more alive. Many others choose to use their money to buy what society should be providing but isn't — for instance, many people send their children to private school, not trusting they can get a good education at the local public school.

What size financial "cushion" do you need for security? Despite their age, Joe (71) and Terry Havens (81) decided to keep only a small emergency fund, just enough to cover a year's modest living expenses. Firmly believing their money was needed in the world (and concerned that the money not be "wasted" on medical care), it felt wrong to them to keep a large personal cushion. George Pillsbury and Mary Tiseo, his wife, decided $500,000 would be their minimum cushion. This will not only be an emergency fund for them and their children, but the income will supplement George's small social change salary, allowing his daily life to be more comfortable and flexible. What do you see as the costs and benefits of keeping a financial cushion? How will you decide what amount seems right? If you have children, what size cushion do you want to pass on to them, if any? (See chapter on Families and Money.)

Is it right to accumulate more wealth? Joseph Collins felt strongly that he couldn't let large sums of money sit in his bank accounts, when every dollar was needed now to right the world and help people in need. Phil Villers feels fine about accumulating wealth; he sees wealth as a terrific vehicle of influence and power he can use to benefit others. How do you feel? If you want to acquire more — for what purposes? How much money do those purposes require? Even the common "accumulation" practice of earning interest was controversial among us: Betsy Duren invested all her money in zero-interest community loans, believing that most interest is payment to the wealthy forced upon ordinary people who need to borrow money for their basic needs. Tracy Gary may agree politically, but she charges some interest when she loans money to community groups, so the pot of money she loans out can grow, or at least cover losses.

*　　　*　　　*　　　*　　　*

"What's my fair share in an unfair world?" Even though there are no exact answers, don't stop asking the question! Look squarely at the injustices, care about them, wrestle honestly with the trade-offs, and come to your own choices. By doing so, you may bring greater integrity to your life, and also gain useful insights to share with others. We're all trying to make sense of this life, negotiating how to move from the world as it is to how we want it to be. Let's help each other.

1. On a postcard from Leeds Postcards, Box 84, Leeds LSI 4HU, England. For more information about Dom Helder Camara, see Hale, May. *The Impossible Dream: The Spirituality of Dom Helder Camara*. Maryknoll, NY: Orbis Books, 1979. Also, Camara, Dom Helder. *The Desert is Fertile*. Maryknoll, NY: Orbis Books.

2. For further discussion of these points we recommend: Rose, Stephen J. *The American Profile Poster: Who Owns What, Who Makes How Much, Who Works Where, & Who Lives with Whom*. New York: Random House, 1986.

3. Greenstein, Robert and Barancik, Scott. *Drifting Apart: New FIndings on Growing Income Disparities Between the Rich, the Poor, and the Middle Class*. Center on Budget and Policy Priorities, Washington D.C., 1990, p. 17, Table A-2.

4. From Table 7 in Avery, Robert B. and Kennickell, Arthur B. "Measurement of Household Savings Obtained from First-Differencing Wealth Estimates." Paper presented at the 21st General Conference of the International Association for Research in Income and Wealth, Lahnstein, FRG, August 20-26, 1989.

5. *Ibid.*

6. *The Economist Book of Vital World Statistics.* New York: Random House, 1990, p. 41.

7. We lacked PPP ratios for some of the countries in the three starred economic groups, so we took the averages of the countries for which data was available.

8. There is a growing number of studies in this area. Three of the classics are: Meadows, Meadows, Randers, and Behrens. *The Limits to Growth.* New York: Universe Books, 1976, Trainer, E.F. *Abandon Affluence!* London: Zed Books, 1985, and Brown, Lester R. *State of the World.* New York: Norton & Co., 1991.

9. Brown, Lester, ibid., p. 156.

10. Audré Lorde, excerpted from a transcript of a commencement speech delivered at Oberlin College, May 29, 1989.

11. These principals were adopted from the book: Gandhi, Mahatma. *Trusteeship.* Ahmedabad, India: Navagivan Publishing House, 1960.

12. Gandhi, Mahatma. *The Essential Gandhi.* Fischer, Louis, ed. New York: Random House, 1962, p. 284.

LIBERATION FOR THE RICH

To be greedy, you must feel that you are alone in some basic way.

— Philip Slater [1]

Liberate the rich?! Surely, of all the groups in the world, we rich people are least in need of "liberation." We seem free to do whatever we want, to have whatever we want, even to be whatever we want!

On one level this is certainly true. The advantages of our wealth are obvious: freedom from financial worries; the option of living in a safe and pleasant environment; opportunities for education; the time and money to enjoy the arts, to think, to read, to travel...But rich people are deeply hurt and limited, emotionally and socially, by systems of economic inequality. Of course, these hurts are on quite a different scale from grinding poverty and the absence of basic rights, but they are still real hurts. When we acknowledge how we've been hurt by the way the social and economic system is set up, we can more clearly see that we rich folks, too, have something to gain from changing the inequities of the class system.

What is the pain of wealthy people like? Since no generalization about groups of people is accurate for every individual, keep in mind that the following is simply a composite picture of hurt and liberation drawn from the lives of many upper-class people. If you gained wealth late in life much of this won't apply. You may recognize only some elements of your life here, less intensely experienced. The basic patterns described here, however, exist in many upper-class families.

As very young children, we assumed that everyone lived as we did. As we grew older, we began to notice differences between our family and others. Why did we have much more than we needed, when others didn't have enough? Sometimes our awakening came by asking about the lives of the people who were paid to care for us: Where did they live? Why did they work so hard and get paid so little? Sometimes it came from noticing the lives of children from other parts of town. However we awakened, we had the natural, instinctive reaction of a child: This is wrong! I don't want to be different from other people!

And how did our families respond to our awakening? Spoken or unspoken, the message was clear: "Don't talk about such things, it's not polite." "Nothing is wrong here — we deserve what we have." In order to keep the love and acceptance of our families — the people we depended on for survival — we had to deny our own perceptions and feelings.

As we grew older, we were surrounded by more of our families' (and society's) attitudes: "We are smarter and better than other people, that's why we're rich." "Anyone can become wealthy if they really want to — people who don't make it are lazy." (But if our parents thought the people they paid to care for us were lazy and stupid and inferior, why were we left with them for long periods of time?) "There's nothing we can do about inequalities so it's fine for us to have all we do." "Anyway, we're not really rich — there are others with lots more." To make sense of how we were different, we wrapped these justifications around us like a protective cloak. If we felt uncomfortable with being born different, we could always fend off the hurt with the myth of superiority. While we may have imaged ourselves superior, we usually felt lonely and isolated, too, afraid of the rest of humanity — and we carried these feelings into adulthood.

On the surface, many of our lives seemed storybook-perfect — summer homes on the lake, fancy schools in idyllic surroundings, riding and music lessons, clothes, cars. We were told we should be grateful and always happy. But underneath, alcoholism, sexual abuse, emotional neglect and ordinary unhappiness were common in our families, just as they are in families of other classes. But the need to keep up appearances was stronger. Who were we to complain — weren't we the privileged ones? So we learned to deny our own reality, to push our pain and anger down, and pretend that everything was fine.

Growing into adulthood brought some of us emotional binds that glued us even further into the system that separates us from others. Many of us with inheritances floundered in our work. On one hand, from our families and elite schools we felt enormous pressures and expectations to succeed. "Don't waste the opportunities your privilege has provided. You should do great things with what you have been given." On the other hand, we had no financial motivation to work and an immobilizing array of choices. The money, which could buy us prestige and influence, became a distorted source of our self-respect. We became more attached to the wealth and our family name...at the cost of knowing our real selves, and what at heart was most important to us.

These scars of classism haunted us as we matured: many of us felt fake and numb beneath the prettiness of our external lives, out of touch with reality and unable to know or express our true selves. We felt lonely and isolated, unable to feel safe, to make close friends, or to feel a part of humanity. We were trapped into covering our pain with attitudes of arrogance and entitlement, which only distanced us further from others.

Classism, like sexism and racism, systematically denies the humanity and flexibility of everyone caught within it. For those of us in the dominant position (men in sexism, whites in racism, the rich in classism), the material rewards we gain from our dominance can easily blind us to how we, too, could benefit from changing the oppressive system. But when we look honestly at the emotional and spiritual emptiness many of us feel in the midst of affluence, we begin to see that ending classism can liberate rich people, too.

*   *   *   *

What are some steps towards liberation? How is it possible to get out of the powerful systems described above? Here are some suggestions, derived from stories of wealthy people who have freed themselves to live closer to their visions. This list summarizes most of the main themes of this book, which are elaborated elsewhere. Keep in mind that each one of the steps takes time and effort. They don't follow any particular order,

and you'll probably invent some additions as you go along, if you undertake this work. We hope you do.

Acknowledge reality and learn about change. Find out where wealth comes from, including your own. Examine the real conditions of poverty, and think critically about the social forces that cause these problems. How do the systems of inequality work? Study how social change comes about. Work towards full awareness of the problems and your ability to act.

Examine the ways you have been hurt by the system of classism as well as how you have benefitted from it. Work on healing your own emotional scars. (In the Resource list, see the Reevaluation Co-counseling Network's work on owning class issues, and the list of professionals who focus on the emotional aspects of wealth.)

Take control over your money. If you have been denied access to information or control over your assets by family, trust officers or other professionals, get help to make your claim and assert your authority. Since money issues are often tied into family power struggles, be sure to get help not only from people with technical competence but also from people who can help you deal with the emotions that may be brought up in confronting family patterns.

Seek new sources of security. Security comes from many sources other than money — from connection with communities of people who share your beliefs; from friendships based on mutual assistance and cooperation; from emotional, physical and spiritual health; from fulfilling work. (See the chapters on Building Security and Finding Meaningful Work.) As you improve these non-material aspects of life, you can reduce your consumption of resources. Make realistic plans for your financial needs and those of your family, and plan ways to reduce your reliance on wealth as a source of security and fulfillment. Most of us consume far more than what we need to be comfortable and far beyond what the world can sustain.

Use your money to support your deepest values. Consider committing significantly more of your money — including assets as well as income — to help

change the world. If you value sharing the power your money brings, experiment with involving people who aren't wealthy in your funding decisions. (See chapter on Sharing Power and Privilege).

Offer your unique strengths. Beyond your financial assets, use time, skills, energy, and access to influence people to work for change. Listen to the voice within, discover groups or issues to work with, and learn how to be of service. You have a lot to offer, much more than just money. Discover a niche that feels right and stay with it over time to make change.

Build alliances across classes. Start by developing one- to-one relationships with people different from yourself. Develop mutual respect by learning about each other's lives and views of the world. Work with organizations that bring people together from various class backgrounds who are dedicated to making a better world, and support the leadership of people from other backgrounds. Build a new sense of community with different types of people.

*   *   *   *   *

What do we have to gain by stepping beyond the limits imposed by our wealth? We can drop the masks and relax — be our true selves, no longer needing to maintain facades. Our children will probably be healthier, less damaged by the isolation, resentment, guilt and confusion that many of us experienced growing up. We won't need to protect ourselves from others less fortunate. (Our country clubs may be lovely — but they are surrounded by high fences to keep out those we fear.) And we have an opportunity to discover a different kind of power — not power over people, but a sense of our own effectiveness and ability to work with others.

Each of us holds a piece of the truth. If we are surrounded only by others like us, our view of the world is severely limited. When we open our lives and work as peers with people of all classes and races, breaking out of our isolation and "coming home" to the wider community, our lives are enriched by a wider set of viewpoints and perspectives — a fuller truth.

Money and wealth divert us from the things we really care about. When we assert our independence from the requirements of maintaining wealth and privilege, we are free to pursue lives dedicated to the liberation of ourselves and others, each of us special but also completely ordinary: a member of the human race.

1. Slater, Philip. *Wealth Addiction*. New York: E.P. Dutton, Inc., 1980, p.159.

BUILDING SECURITY

Teresina provides a beautiful example of inner security. She knows what her capacities are and believes in them. She can embody those values in what she does and in the way she lives. That's security. It's utterly different from financial security. It's the security of satisfaction, of knowing one has lived a good life.

— Joe Havens

However much money or power we have, most of us struggle to feel secure in an insecure world. We are constantly bombarded — by advertisers, insurance companies, TV, newspapers, well-meaning friends and relatives — with anxiety about the uncertainties of life. We are taught that the only defense against disaster is to build up a sturdy wall of financial assets.

Money provides security because many basic institutions which traditionally provided security — extended families, neighborhoods, and religious organizations — have broken down. (In times past, for example, if a family's breadwinner became disabled, neighbors or church members could be counted on to help.) In addition, the United States (unlike most western countries) provides frighteningly few safety nets for its citizens. The country has no national health insurance, very limited unemployment insurance, a minimum wage too low to live on, a regressive tax system with few supports for working parents, little effective legislation to stop plant shutdowns and runaway shops, meager social security allotments, and inadequate pension systems. No wonder people feel insecure! Without these structures, families and individuals must fend for themselves, and this society tells us the surest way to do that is by obtaining wealth. Yet in the push to get richer, our inner sense of security diminishes instead of building.

> In our country, people are freer than ever to amass great wealth, but they are also freer to fail, and without solid kin or friendship networks, failure can spell disaster. So we have inherited a succeed-or-starve mentality in which success depends on the individual's personal ambition, competitiveness, and discipline. And behind the will to succeed is the ever- present worry that the market will shift or a competitor will get an edge and suddenly all will be lost. Psychologically, capitalism is driven as much by fear as by the profit motive. [1]

Moreover, for those of us who are wealthy — and perhaps especially for the very rich — fears do not go away because we have more. They change from one kind of fear (e.g., not being able to pay the rent) to another kind (e.g., not being loved for who we are). For some of the very rich who focus their entire lifetimes on accumulating wealth, amassing assets can become an obsession, a vicious circle that never provides the sought-after security. Says sociologist Philip Slater:

> The rich...come to feel that no one cares for them—only for their money....They therefore need very badly to control and coerce it [their affection]. But the more they do, the less they can trust what they get. Money can be trusted, of course, but it doesn't satisfy the need. The more money, the less trust; the less trust, the more money. . .Even their children cannot be trusted, for if they are at all like their parents—trusting only in money—they are waiting anxiously for them [their parents] to die. [2]

Very rich "wealth addicts" (as Slater calls people who take wealth-seeking to an extreme) are the most trapped in this cycle, but we are all part of a society that emphasizes developing wealth to the neglect of other sources of security. Some observers of U.S. life, especially those from the Third World, have suggested that although American society is a highly "developed" nation in the sense of material affluence, it is spiritually underdeveloped and is becoming socially underdeveloped. We seem to have gained monetary wealth by impoverishing our lives in other ways.

> *   *   *   *   *

Many of us would like to discover a healthy balance between money and other parts of our lives. If we were less dependent on amassing more money in an elusive search for security, we could be freer to use our money and lives in other ways. Let's look carefully at what we mean by security and how each of us can develop strength and confidence from an array of sources:

Take control of your finances. Many people (wealthy or not) feel ongoing anxiety about money because they're never sure how much they actually need. Once you have a clearer picture of your finances, it becomes easier to imagine and create sources of security not related to money.

Keep careful track of expenses for three to six months — to see how you actually spend money. Then total and assess those expenditures: is this the way you want to use your money? Try making a realistic yearly budget. (See the financial planning exercise in the Appendix.) Any surprises?

Experiment with making some projected long-term budgets, planning for things you desire and those you fear. How much money would you need to travel through Asia after retirement? How much might supporting your aging parents for ten years cost? Since types of insurance exist to protect against almost any financial burden (e.g. losing your sight, becoming disabled, requiring at-home nursing care), research the cost of insurance for risks you face and plan it into your budget.

If this type of planning is too difficult, technically or emotionally, try investing in the services of a professional financial planner. Peace of mind is worth the effort — figuring out current and expected expenses and planning how to meet them can be a key step towards feeling centered and secure.

Heal yourself. Many of us grew up in families where we didn't feel safe and weren't loved. Those of us who carry these early wounds may have trouble feeling secure no matter what our financial circumstances. Invest in your healing. Work with a therapist, participate in peer counseling classes, attend personal growth seminars, reflect deeply on your life with the help of good books and friends. Whatever methods you choose, healing yourself will enable you to experience more love, confidence and self-respect. Without these, you will carry holes in your heart that no amount of money can fill.

Rely more on yourself and more on others. Security develops with a good balance of these apparent opposites. How balanced is your life? The dominant culture hypes self-reliance: "Stand on your own two feet! Don't depend on other people." But despite this emphasis, few of us learn many skills of self- reliance. Those of us with money are particularly prone to buying services rather than doing practical things ourselves. Developing new skills may strengthen your sense of security — repairing things that break in your home, tuning your own car, taking care of simple medical problems. If you have always lived on inherited money, try earning your living for a while. If you always need company on Saturday night, learn the pleasure of being with yourself.

On the other hand, because our culture emphasizes autonomy, many of us have weak support networks. Deep and caring friendships and family ties can be a primary source of security. These are the people who will help if your car breaks down, watch your kids so you can go to the store, listen to your troubles, and let you know you are loved. No stock portfolio can do that, no matter how large it is.

> My father said,..."I've said this before, but I want to say it again. When you need me I will be here. I'll drop whatever I'm doing if you are in trouble or sick."
>
> — Chuck Collins

Review the state of your relationships. Day to day, do others help you? Do you help them? Just as earning money takes time, building mutually supportive relationships takes an investment of energy and interest. You may want to re-contact friends and family members with whom you've been out of touch. You may need to resolve old conflicts, or take new risks to deepen your communication with them. Experiment with asking for help in small ways.

You can also build greater security by becoming a valued part of a wider community — a neighborhood association or social club, a labor union or alumni group, a music group or car pool, or a group based on shared values and vision for the world.

> I feel my long-term security within the larger community of the peace movement. I feel very secure in this sense of community and in a life given in good part to service.
>
> — Nelia Sargent

Within these wider circles, you can experiment with ways to build each other's security. Community gardens, land trusts, mutual aid funds, and systems where people barter to exchange goods and services all help to build relationships of mutual support which benefit everyone. (See *How to Prepare for the Coming Depression* by Mark Friedman and *How to Make a Better World* by Jeffrey Hollender.)

Increase your physical security. How well do you eat, exercise, rest, deal with stress, and take care of yourself when you're ill? Again, building good health takes an investment of energy, particularly if you have habits to unlearn, but few other things are as important.

Your physical environment also affects your well-being. Many people are discovering that symptoms they have put up with for years disappear when they remove the hidden toxins in their homes. (The book *Non-Toxic, Natural and Earth-wise* by Debra Dadd describes how to do this.) If you live in the heart of a stressful city, you may even find that the best way to increase your security is to move to a cleaner and safer location.

Feed your spirit. Read about people or movements which inspire you. Pursue spiritual experiences that have meaning for you. Discover how to tap sources of beauty, strength, and love inside yourself and beyond — through meditation, prayer, creativity, nature, solitude, service — whatever works for you.

You may find it difficult to integrate these practices into your life, especially if you haven't made room for them before. It often helps to start small. Instead of aiming to meditate a half hour a day and failing, experiment with ten-minute meditations a couple of times a week. If nature moves you, a single flower on your desk may serve as an easy-to-achieve spiritual reminder, while a week's trip to the Rockies might be more desirable but out of reach. Pursue practices like these as play, not work. Ask friends where they derive their daily inspiration and try out their ideas. Find fellow seekers who can support your growth.

Many people's deepest insecurity comes from their fear of aging, death and loss — fears deeply reinforced by the dominant culture. No amount of money will prevent your skin from sagging or your loved ones from dying, although many people try to bury their fears with face lifts, health spas, and relentless buying. Fears of death are much better soothed by experiencing fulfillment in our lives and by developing a spiritual acceptance of life's endless changes.

Help build our collective security. Many of our deepest fears and insecurities arise from the awareness that we live in a dangerous world on the brink of social, nuclear, and environmental catastrophe. We also live in a dangerous country, within a system that allows massive poverty, homelessness and unemployment. No matter how carefully planned your finances or how wide your support network, no matter how fit your body or how enlightened your spirit, you live and breathe within these fundamental national and global insecurities.

When you work with others to create a better collective future, you change from being a passive victim of impending disaster to an active supporter of life. Add your talents to those working for universal health care, or progressive tax structures, or a dignified minimum wage. Work with your local recycling group, or help teach conflict-resolution in schools, or lobby Congress for a reduced military budget. While you may not see many changes in this lifetime, you will be fueled with more energy and hope by knowing you are helping to build a more secure world for generations to come.

* * * * *

Many of us spend our lifetimes trying to hide from a vague sense of insecurity, rarely stopping to examine our fears and what we might do about them. Haunted by unnamed but numerous anxieties, those of us with extra money usually hold on to it for the future, feeling, "I need this for protection. You just never know what's going to happen."

But with courage and support we can face our fears and look squarely at the underlying needs. "I'm scared I'll be alone and unlovable when I'm old." "I'm afraid college costs will be so astronomical my children won't be able to go." Equipped with this clarity, we can take practical steps toward creating more security — by managing our finances, developing our emotional and physical health, building loving relationships, and creating more sources of meaning and purpose in our lives. When we are fortified with well-rounded sources of security, we will find ourselves more free to use our resources in new and meaningful ways.

1. Schwartz, Richard. "The American Nightmare" In *The Family Therapy Networker*, March/April 1991, p. 66.

2. Slater, Philip, *Wealth Addiction*. New York: Dutton, 1983, p. 102.

CHARLES GRAY

Charles, 64, has worked as a sociology professor and organizer. He has not only given away all his wealth, but has chosen a very simple lifestyle which reflects his values.

My family was poor by U.S. standards, while my former wife, Leslie, was from the upper class. But love conquers all they say! So I married and changed class.

I was always concerned with the maldistribution of the world's wealth, and Leslie had pretty much the same feelings. We used the income from Leslie's wealth to fund peace, justice, civil liberties, and environmental movements. We started resisting 100% of our income taxes in 1972, because no matter what we pay, at least half of it goes to militarism, and much of the balance goes toward programs that perpetuate an unjust socio-economic order. Although the IRS eventually seized money from our bank account, it still felt worthwhile not to pay voluntarily.

Having wealth through my former wife significantly affected my life; I never had to worry about paying a bill. We could fall back on the fortune for whatever we needed, like education, or for when we couldn't find meaningful work or wanted to do volunteer work instead of earning money. Occasionally, it made friends envious. When I was young and insecure, having wealth made me feel important. However, when I was older it decreased my self-esteem because I was ashamed that I had not redistributed it.

We began to feel that global crises required a greater investment. After years of rather eclectic giving and searching for the "perfect" project, we decided that unless we expended our assets now, we might be too late to stop the rush to oblivion. Sitting on capital is crazy when it is five minutes to midnight. So we put a substantial part of our fortune into the hands of a group of people we had worked with in the peace and justice movements in the Pacific Northwest. The group decided to use our money to create the McKenzie River Gathering Foundation. Leslie and I specified that the money go to projects in the Northwest United States that were consistent with nonviolent philosophy and that did not produce revenue for the U.S. government.

As a sociologist I began to do research on resource and income distribution among people around the world. Strongly believing that everyone on the earth has a right to an equal share of the resources of this planet, I decided that I would no longer live on more than my share. So I worked out what I call the World Equity Budget, which is a rough calculation of what each person's share would be if the world's yearly income were shared equally. I used the 1960 Gross World Product as an estimate of a sustainable economy and divided that by current population estimates to get an approximation of my share. It came to about $960 per person per year in 1977.

When I decided to live on this budget, I felt definitely way out by myself. I had to make a choice between moving a few inches with others or moving a hundred feet alone. The motivation was a moral imperative: I had no right to continue living on stolen property. It was like a religious belief. My models were Gandhi, Jesus, Kagowa, Dorothy Day, Tolstoy. Like them, I personally could feel the injustice of wealth. I felt the oppression of the Third World, imagining hungry children and my part in that hunger. I believed that God's gifts should be shared equally.

For years I felt seduced to keep wealth for myself and my own goals. It never seemed to be quite the right time to give it away or return it to those from whom it was taken. My former wife and I lived on her fortune to do work we thought was important in the world. But using the money for good ends didn't answer the question of whether we had a moral and legitimate right to have power over those resources. I could no longer support choosing to hold on to that power. I felt, as a privileged person, I needed to really join the poor and struggle.

Before entering into this new life, I hadn't kept close track of my expenditures, but I estimate I lived on about $3,500 a year. It took me seven months to reduce my consumption so that I could live within the World Equity Budget. I gave away everything I owned except for some personal things like clothing. Over a three-year period I gave away 99.8% of my wealth, keeping what I thought was reasonable savings for a low-income person of age 53. I have maintained savings since ranging from $500 to $2,000.

For the two years I was making this decision and beginning to reduce my consumption, my wife and I struggled over our differences. Leslie's strategy was one of institutional change, and mine was a strategy of institutional change coupled with personal example. We got on each other's nerves; we couldn't live together in the same household with such different lifestyles. Leslie's lifestyle was modest by U.S. standards, but mine, by the same standards, was extreme. We separated in 1977, but have remained good friends, held together by our common interests and by our two children.

So I began living in what some people call "voluntary poverty" — although I don't consider my fair share to be poverty. I rented a small room, stopped eating in restaurants or going to paid entertainment unless someone treated me (I later stopped accepting treats), biked and hitchhiked for transportation, and wore second-hand clothes. I scrounged food from garbage. The budget allowed me $78.40 a month, but soon I was averaging $47 a month because I wanted to save. I would kid with some of my friends who couldn't save or were getting into debt. "Charles, you're saving more than we are," they would chuckle or grumble. With some of my savings I helped establish a small emergency fund with several other non-wealthy friends that we all can draw on if necessary. This helps my security, but Leslie and I realized back when we gave away lots of money that real security comes from people loving us and taking care of us in times of need.

When I started living on the World Equity Budget, I wrote a letter to all of my friends, explaining my thinking. "My goal," I said, "is to personally live in such a way that I am neither controlling nor using more than my share of the world's wealth. My motivation is based on the belief that for us to have any reasonable chance of a peaceful society, the maldistribution of the world's wealth must be ended. That maldistribution is extreme. In the mid 1980s the richer industrialized nations, about 16% of the world's people, have per-capita annual gross national products (GNPs) ranging from $3000 to $6500. In contrast, the majority of the world's people live in countries whose per-capita annual GNP ranges from $75 to $250. Imagine trying to live on $250 a year. Fifty-five percent of the people of the world live on less than that!"

This unjust status quo is maintained by investments in military power, by tanks and missiles. The high-consumption lifestyle we have become used to in the rich nations is protected by the threat and actual use of massive violence. Thus, if we want to renounce violence, we must renounce the maldistribution of wealth as well.

If global wealth were redistributed equally, it would give the majority of the people of this earth more than five times the income they have today. Imagine what a boon to humanity that would be — what a blossoming of hope, joy, love and peace that might produce! And so, as an answer to increasing violence, I strive for the equal sharing of the fruits of this blessed green earth. I now believe that a "rich pacifist" is a contradiction in terms.

I've been living on the budget consistently since 1977. Since I remarried in 1982, my wife Dorothy has lived within the budget too. Dorothy made a more drastic transition than I did to live on the World Equity Budget. In one month she went from a well-paying job in nursing administration, with a house and a car, to living on $1,000 a year. But she had decided a long time before that when her son graduated from high school, she would devote her life to living simply and to serving the poor. While she had no formula in mind, her dream was very compatible with mine.

Our combined income is about $250 a month. Although it may not sound like much money, we are still in the upper one-third of the people in the world. We have felt good about what we're doing. It has been a very interesting experience, and we've learned a few tricks about how to survive. We try not to lay a guilt trip on our friends, but we do feel the world would be a lot better off if a lot more people did what we're doing.

We make our living mostly on weekends — doing nursing, janitorial work, and gardening for our bread money. Several years ago, we were both deeply engaged in the Fast for Life as fast organizers, and we each accepted $60 a month for our full-time work. Dorothy started nursing again after the Fast for Life. She accepts the standard hourly pay of the conventional institutions she works in, but I set my own wages, based on what I call the World Equity Wage. In determining this wage, I chose what I considered a fair and adequate amount of work for each person to contribute to society: fifty hours per month. I divide fifty hours a month into the World Equity Budget (which is now up to $132 a month) and get $2.64 an hour.

The physical part of living on this budget is actually not so hard. In such a wasteful society it's easy to live on the waste. I've discovered more people doing this than I'd realized. Dorothy and I consume less and enjoy it more. We still need celebrations and treats, of course, but we've learned that sharing an ice cream cone can be as satisfying as sharing a fancy dinner.

Currently we live pretty comfortably in a nine-by-ten foot room in a house. We built a loft, and have a desk under the bed. The owner rents to us on a non-profit basis. We don't think we should be subsidized, but we don't see this as a subsidy. Housing should be non-profit, and we pay our share of house bills, given our space. Our monthly rent is $165, of which we pay $65 in labor on the house. I'm starting to build a shelter at the back of the house, which we won't have to pay for, which will cut down on our costs and labor time.

Using resources equitably is not just a matter of how much you spend, but on what you spend it. In 1981, I changed the budget to give "credit" — that is, to allow us to spend more — for products produced locally, cooperatively, or in an ecologically sound manner. These are often higher priced than products produced with petroleum or imported by a multinational corporation paying slave wages to workers in other countries. Our "Eco-dollar" budget is now $132/month/person.

I have a limit on accepting gifts. People have tried to subsidize us—offering housing at greatly reduced rates, for instance — but if anything looks like a subsidy, we have to refuse it. If we are going to live on our share we've got to live on our share.

Some of our friends feel guilty comparing themselves to us. They feel our action is a judgment of their lifestyle — which it is, in a way. When some people are starving and others have more than they need, it's not right. We talk very little about what we're doing, but it's obvious it's in their minds. For example, when one couple bought a car, they felt like they had to justify it to us.

I think it's good for people to feel responsible for conditions in the world, but I don't push people very much; I know they have to find their own way. I feel sad about that, because those starving to death can't afford that much time. However, I come from a liberal background, and liberals are very tolerant. I'm also a coward; I don't want to push too hard and lose all my friends. And pushing doesn't usually have a very positive effect. Everyone has to come to his or her own decisions in his or her own time and manner.

I don't want people to feel guilty — I want them to increase in awareness and sensitivity. I want people to change their lives, to adopt right living. Our intent in doing this personal witness is modelling our lives to be consistent with the reality we see — hoping our example will move others to live more consistently with that reality. Our witness is not simply that we gave up some privilege, but also that we try to live day to day, as equals of the other peoples of the world.

Taking this stand is often lonely. People haven't exactly been lining up at the door to adopt the World Equity Budget. The most painful part has been how it has affected relationships to loved ones. It cost me some close friendships, and led to the breakup of my first marriage after 31 years. Ideally, I would have liked to have found a more complete consensus with my former wife and prevented the ending of our marriage. But this life choice has also led to new close friendships, including my second marriage.

I have done my most important work since I have been poor. I now feel close to the issues of the unemployed and the homeless because I am close to living that way myself. Awareness of the reality of poverty continually motivates me to do more about injustice. If I were living my old lifestyle, my work for social justice would be more intellectual, less immediate.

All things considered, I do not think I could have done it differently. Ideally I would have done it much sooner, but we didn't have the analysis of the connection between our wealth and others' poverty. Some of us are slow learners.

Giving away principal was a profound emotional experience. I experienced struggle and joy, and both were positive. Materially, it certainly lightened my pack, and I certainly have had to be a little more creative to survive. But spiritually, I have been immensely relieved. I feel I have rejoined the human race.

NELIA SARGENT

Nelia is a 35-year-old activist from an old Quaker family. She has worked as a nonviolence trainer in the anti-nuclear movement, and is a graduate student in music.

Some money in my family came from my father's publishing company, Porter and Sargent, but much of it dates back to earlier generations. My father's side of the family included lawyers and engineers, and we also had a machine tool company. My mother comes from a comfortable background; her father was a country doctor. He delivered babies on kitchen tables, with chickens running around underneath, and didn't get paid half of the time.

My grandfather, although too old for military service, was an outspoken opponent of World War I. My father was a pacifist and a conscientious objector during World War II. My mother worked for the military as a decoder during World War II, but right after that she joined the peace movement. In 1960 both my parents were at the conference of the Peacemakers where the Community for Nonviolent Action (CNVA) was formed. This group was a strong influence throughout my childhood.

My parents also resisted the federal phone tax (imposed to pay for war debt), but because my father's business was in his name, he couldn't become a complete war tax resister without risking losing the two-generation-old company. He was a publisher who used the profits from publishing private-school directories to finance publication of ideas that needed to be heard. Sometimes my father was teased about that side of the publishing house — people would call it "deficit publishing." Sometimes those books accidentally made money, but that was not why he took them on.

My family was non-traditional, a large extended household with international guests and street people often coming through. The Boston branch of CNVA was also based with us during its short existence. Within this extended household and family, I was taught to question some of the traditional economic values of our society. In fact, the only strong disagreement I had with my parents in adolescence was on the question of their life insurance. When I was in high school, my dad opened a bank account for me in which he would deposit payments for his life insurance. I had to sign these four times a year, and it often took him three or four days to gain my cooperation. We talked the issues through: I explained to my father that I loved and respected him, that I wanted *him* and not his money, and that I would give away this money someday. He understood that; he didn't take it as a personal rejection or affront — it was fine with him if I made that decision after he died.

He died when I was 20, the year I also became legally blind. I had been losing my sight for three years due to *retinitis pigmentosa*—freckles on the retina. When I received the money from my father's life insurance, I immediately loaned it anonymously for five years to several peace and justice groups. I intended to turn the loans into grants at the end of the five years, but since I was only 20 at the time and conventional wisdom was so opposed to what I was doing, I gave myself room to change my mind.

I gave to groups that had as low an overhead and did as much service as possible. I wasn't particularly systematic, but simply chose groups I'd been familiar with since childhood. One group I gave to was the Institute for Community Economics. I didn't track the money's effectiveness — just deciding where it would go felt like a lot of power. Once I chose groups I simply let go. I didn't feel it was my money that they were using, I was just channeling it.

I was very pleased five years later to terminate those loans and to turn them into gifts. Now, at the age of 35, 15 years after giving it away, I don't regret giving the money at all. I would do the same thing again without hesitation.

My mother has since cancelled her own life insurance policy, I'm delighted to say. I'm very easy to get along with, I think, until it runs into principles, and then I'm very stubborn!

*   *   *   *   *

I found a very deep inner peace by choosing to give the money away, live simply, and not participate in the oppression of others. The violence of traditional economics was more than I was able to stomach, and I wanted no more part of it. For me, the connection between "the haves" and "the have-nots" was never "out of sight, out of mind." It was clear that because some people have more resources than they need, other people never have enough. The knowledge of this connection caused me a lot of anguish. For instance, as we talk we sit on property that has been in my family for generations, a place I see as being built by the blood, sweat, and tears of a lot of the local workers. We have more land than anyone should ever have, and I feel it is immoral.

We're not Rockefellers, of course, and this fertile agricultural land can't be compared to the vast encroachment of industry. Our family has protected the woods and about a dozen species of very rare plants, so our owning it has not been all negative. I went through a long period of wishing that I could turn this property into a community land trust, but that's out of the question. It's owned jointly by lots of cousins and there's no hope of getting everyone's agreement.

I spent twelve years trying to deny my economic class. It was a ridiculous exercise — I mean, who was I fooling? It wasn't honest to myself or anyone else. But I tried to be as unhypocritical as I could. I didn't live a modest lifestyle, and then go on fancy vacations — I lived without much money all of the time. It was by choice, though, and now I clearly recognize that choosing simplicity is very different from being forced into poverty.

I now accept that I am who I am, including my class background. I recognize that if people want to blame me for what I was born into, that's their problem, not mine. I do hold myself responsible for what I choose to make of that background today, and I believe very strongly in doing that.

When I decided to give my money away, I couldn't talk about it at all with most of my extended family, many of whom are quite wealthy and conservative. Even one set of cousins, who are armchair radicals — they don't do much politically, but are in political agreement with me — worried that I was compromising my security by giving the money away. I didn't know the answers to their security-related questions. I just knew I could not participate in that kind of monetary gain and live with myself comfortably. I had to give up my wealth to gain inner peace.

In terms of security needs around my blindness, I was very lucky. I spent six months at a training program which provides independent living skills for blind adults. That gave me the tools to continue what my spirit wanted — an independent existence. Before that I'd had the will, but not the tools. The training experience made it clear to me that I could continue to do pretty much anything I wanted to, although the way in which I participated might be altered. For example, I don't ski downhill alone any more, but I do ski with a partner, and I ski alone cross-country. Blindness has been a real nuisance, but rarely a handicap.

I discovered an unexpected security issue when I lived in my family house. One side of the house is like an 1850 museum, and while I lived there something happened which horrified me, something I had observed in some of my wealthier cousins: I began to feel fearful of people because I had things that could be taken. That gave me a terrible sense of insecurity. I have found much more security by being free from that kind of wealth. Now there is nothing in the apartment I live in worth taking. We didn't even have a lock on the door the first four years I was there — a wonderful freedom.

My basic sense of security has less to do with having material resources and more to do with feeling part of an extended family — that is, the peace movement family. I feel very secure in this sense of community, and in a life given in good part to service. It has proven true for me over and over again that everything given is returned a hundredfold.

Until this last year, I have been supporting myself by caning chairs. Making my living this way was useful, while I juggled my schedule to do anti-nuclear work. I could cane at six in the morning or at midnight. It was a privilege to be in the right place at the right time to work with the Clamshell Alliance against nuclear power, but I can't foresee doing organizing at quite that intensity anymore. I no longer thrive in crisis scenarios, though I am open to high risk situations for limited time periods, such as when I went down to the war zone in Nicaragua with Witness for Peace.

In this nuclear age we must develop alternatives to violence. I believe we fall back on violence largely for lack of choices and options. My work as a trainer has been to expand people's range of choices of how to deal with conflict. While most of the training in nonviolence has been in the context of civil disobedience, I am interested in a much fuller range of daily applications: from intervening to prevent rape to international conflict resolution. I would like most to be doing public speaking about the practical applications of nonviolence and training people (including police and municipal officials) in-depth in the techniques of nonviolence. I think about working with professor Gene Sharp who has done extensive research and public speaking on the history and strategy of non-violent action.

I am at an elite New England school, Smith College, because I recognize the credibility that a piece of paper like a diploma from Smith can give. I want to have influence at as many levels as I can reach, including with middle- and upper-class people. I'm not interested in scrambling to gain access to power and privilege, but I am now willing to use the influence I have by virtue of my family and upbringing. I think I can be more effective using the privilege rather than denying it. It has been healing for me to come full circle, to return to my background after having denied it for so long.

The kind of self-acceptance I feel now has just emerged in the last few years. I still haven't spoken publicly about money issues, because, for so long, I had tried hard to deny that I had money. When I went on the Continental Walk for disarmament and social justice in 1976 I made a point of not even mentioning my last name, because it seemed that everyone I kept running into— all the elders in the peace movement—knew my family.

Being quiet about giving away the money felt funny because I definitely believed I was doing it as a witness, and that eventually I would want people to know. But I didn't want any barrier to common equality. I didn't want people coming to me with funding requests — I didn't want to deal with that inequality at all.

* * * * *

I acknowledge my own needs now in a way that I was not able to before. I was impressed by something Slow Turtle, a medicine man of the Wampanoag Nation once said: "It's important to include ourselves in the circle of those we care for." This is my goal. But not to favor myself. I still live simply, although no longer on the $4,000 per year that I used to live on — it's probably twice that now, plus tuition. I continue to give away more than half of the income I receive from the family trust fund. Part of caring for myself includes fun and play. Making music with friends is part of sustaining myself in a non-injurious manner; jet-setting around the world, however, is injurious and much more resource intensive.

People ask me whether guilt played a part in my decision. Sure, it was probably a key motivating factor that gave me the impetus to do something, when I might easily have done nothing. So I wouldn't say, "Don't act out of guilt." But I think you do have to go beyond guilt before you make final choices.

I know that some people can get paralyzed by guilt; that's part of what goes on with some members of my family. You can sit around in your pity pot of guilt and not do anything; that doesn't help you or anybody else. Or you can move beyond that stage into action. It's action that has maintained my serenity, both in terms of the threat of nuclear weapons blowing up the whole world, and in terms of class economics. I might not attain perfection by taking action, but at least it's progress. So I encourage other people to do something — it doesn't matter how small the step — to keep moving towards their ideals.

CHUCK COLLINS

Chuck, age 31, is the director of technical assistance at the Institute for Community Economics (I.C.E.). He is often on the road helping low-income community groups set up community land trusts and housing coops.

My great-grandfather was a meat packer who developed a successful recipe for wieners. His name was Oscar Mayer. Oscar opened a little butcher shop in Chicago. The butcher shop expanded, and he moved to Madison, Wisconsin, where he opened a plant which grew even more. Oscar's daughter, Frieda, was a voice student at the Chicago Conservatory of Music. She married an Irish Bohemian musician, Edward Collins, and they had four children, including one who later became my father.

I was born in Madison, the oldest of three children. My father worked at the Oscar Mayer headquarters, and we knew that the Oscar Mayer label was family, part of us. Before I was five, we moved to an old farm in a very affluent suburb of Detroit. I had a lot of friends and, for the most part, a fun childhood.

When I was seven, in the summer of 1967, two things stood out for me. One was learning about baseball and becoming a fan of the Detroit Tigers. The other was having the city erupt into riots. Every day I'd come home, open the newspaper, look at pictures of burning buildings and the National Guard, and then turn to the sports section to read about my baseball heroes. When I went to Tiger Stadium, in a largely Black part of the city, I could feel the fear around me. I noticed that poor people tended to be Black, like our housekeeper, Mrs. Rice, who came from downtown Detroit to work at our house.

Every Friday I'd sit on the couch and look through the latest issue of Life magazine. I was haunted by the faces of the people in the photos I clipped from the magazine — pictures about urban poverty and the Vietnam War. I'll never forget the image of dogs attacking people in the Civil Rights movement, even though I didn't understand what it was all about at the time.

At the private school I attended, my fifth grade class took part in Earth Day. With our science teacher, Mrs. Hawksley, we dug up trash that had been scattered along the road. I was very impressed. My father, a strong environmentalist who had done a lot of hiking with me, helped me write my first leaflet. It said at the top, "Don't throw this paper away—it will cause pollution." My father typed and copied my short article, and then I took it around to all the houses in the neighborhood — about 70. Neighbors said to me for days afterwards, "I really liked that!" I was surprised and pleased—my first social change project.

When I was 16, my father and I drove to Northern Michigan. We had a man-to-man talk, and he told me that I was going to inherit money. He said this inheritance would be a tremendous resource and a privilege. I could use it for my education and to advance and improve my life; it was enough so that I would not have to work if I chose not to. Nevertheless, he said, he hoped that the money would not change me or my life goals. I felt both excitement and dread. This was amazing and wonderful!

I was the only member of my high school class not to go on immediately to college following graduation. That summer I worked on an assembly line in my father's factory. I'm sure people held back, never yelling at me because I was the boss's kid. Even though it was summertime and we'd been in the factory all day, everybody used to eat lunch indoors. Except me — during my half-hour lunch break I would sit on the loading dock in the sun and read. This separated me from people, and once a woman came up to me and said, "You think you're better than us, don't you?" I felt surprised, upset and defensive. I said, "I just don't want to sit inside, and I want to read William Faulkner." I was aware that these were not the only differences between us.

In the fall I went to Worcester, Massachusetts, for a year's internship program at a crisis intervention center. This was the first time I had lived in a city and I wanted to see how other people lived. I felt free being away from home and wanted to explore everything. I lived in a household with two other young men who didn't have much money, made a lot of friends very different from me, and fell in love with somebody who was working class and Jewish. I learned from all those relationships that as much as I wanted to be just like everybody else, I should never underestimate the extent to which my life experience was different.

Later I worked for the Voter Education Project, knocking on doors to get people to register to vote — it was hard, because of how powerless people felt. I also tried to organize public housing tenants, again knocking on doors; people lived in housing that was poorly maintained, and they, too, felt powerless to do anything about it. I began to realize how hard it would be for poor people to stop being poor. Meanwhile, I could see that people of privilege my own age felt that the sky was the limit.

I talked to my boss about how weird it felt to have so much money. He encouraged me to talk to George Pillsbury, an heir to the flour fortune who had recently helped found the Haymarket People's Fund in Boston. When I called George he invited me to a conference for people with inherited wealth. In the introductions, I was amazed to hear the participants say the names of the corporations where their money came from. For the first time I stated aloud, to a room full of people, my connection to Oscar Mayer!

We saw a film called "Controlling Interests" which showed how multi-national corporations control a lot of the Third World. I was excited that a lot of the people in the room had funded the film. I thought, "Wow! That's power!" Then I realized that I, too, could give money to support the production of films like this. After the conference I sent off a check to fund a couple of films I had talked about with George.

When I turned 21, I began giving away the income I had started receiving from my trust to various political organizations, especially to the Haymarket Fund. I agreed with Haymarket's philosophy that decision-making about the use of the money should lie with people who knew the needs of their communities, not with philanthropists. I believed in the Haymarket motto "change not charity," and liked its emphasis on funding grassroots social change organizations.

*   *   *   *   *

Over the next six years I worked for the Institute for Community Economics, helping to build a movement of community-based institutions made up of community land trusts, housing cooperatives, community loan funds, credit unions, and worker cooperatives. I travelled and assisted about 60 groups a year, and saw first-hand that the reason poor communities are poor has nothing to do with the people who live in them, nor with any defect of race or class. In Appalachia I saw that the land is owned mostly by absentee corporate landlords. In Maine I learned that 75% of the land is owned or controlled by out-of-state interests, particularly paper companies and tourist businesses. These experiences made me angry. Why are some people allowed to take things that belong to all of us? Land and natural resources are God-given, and the community should control them. What makes people poor is that they put their labor into something, and don't get much back. What makes people rich is that they keep for themselves value that was created through other people's labor, value that was created by the whole community.

I began to see clearly that my inherited wealth came from this same system. My family owned a company. Our company would buy little piggies from farmers who had raised them, and workers in the company would slaughter them and make them into sausages. The workers created value with their labor and with little piggies. They would get paychecks, but most of the value would flow to the stockholders—including my family and me. Some of that money was invested in other stocks, bonds, or real estate, so we could gain even more money. I discovered that this money, too, ultimately came from the people who had to borrow my money — and to pay interest on it — so they could meet their basic human needs. Over the course of several years, with much thinking and talking with friends, I resolved to give away the bulk of my inheritance.

*   *   *   *   *

I wrote to my father about my plans to give away my money. The night I got back to Massachusetts from Detroit, he called. "I got your letter and I'd really like to talk with you about it. Is there some way we could get together?" I said, "You know, I'm moving on this quickly." He said he understood and he flew into Boston where we met at his hotel.

I felt nervous. He started off: "I'm very, very concerned about this. I really appreciate your letter." He was genuine. He said he had spent some time talking with my stepmother about it. I felt relieved and grateful that he'd thought about how to respond in a caring way. "I don't expect that I am going to dissuade you," he continued. "However, I want to know for myself that you have thought about certain things. I'm not worried about you. You'll manage—you'll be resourceful. I'm concerned about future children. Raising children is expensive. I have spent *at least* a million dollars raising three children. At least! Maybe two or three!"

Now I thought that was a little bit off, but that is what it was to him. He went on: "Even raising your children in a simpler way costs a lot; you can't imagine what it will cost! What if you have a child who has Down's Syndrome? Think about the cost of the care. Until you have children you will never have to grapple with certain elements of reality."

"You know that my lover's parents raised six children," I pointed out, "and her father never made more than $10,000 a year. The children are well-adjusted, with an incredible sense of security, and self-confidence. They don't feel limited. Other friends I know well have also raised children with little money, and it has not been detrimental."

I heard some hurt and anger in my father's voice: "You know I made sacrifices to give that money to you!" I said, "I know and I appreciate your generosity! I'm grateful for some of the opportunities I had as a result of my economic privilege. Money does make a difference. I'm glad I was able to attend good schools, travel, explore the outdoors, and choose meaningful work. Even if I give my money away, I will keep many of the benefits of growing up with economic privilege. It's time for me to put the money to use to benefit others in greater need."

My father said, "I don't want to talk about the politics of wealth. I don't want to talk about the big questions. I'm concerned about you and your inability to live with any paradox in your life!"

I thought to myself, "It's a virtue that I don't accept certain paradoxes of injustice. I don't pretend that all the contradictions will go away. I have to live with some, but others I can do something about!"

"I can appreciate this as a personal action," he said. "But I know you are a social change leader and I want to know if you have a political agenda. If you want to lead some kind of Marxist revolution, this is doubtless a good political move. You're renouncing your class background to be a public leader in a Marxist revolution!"

I have told my father repeatedly, "Dad, you have to understand, I am not a Marxist, and I am not out to preach class warfare. You can call me a Gandhian or a Christian. I would even accept other labels." But my father stuck with his version of the red nightmare: my son, the revolutionary leader who has to renounce his class privilege.

However, over the course of two days with my Dad I responded to many of his concerns and his "what if" questions. A turning point in the conversation came when he asked me to tell him what experiences led me to this decision. So I told him of my development, my understanding of the struggles of working class friends, friendships I had made that really affected me, what I had learned in years of working for the Institute of Community Economics.

By the end of the conversation, he let me know that he didn't exactly bless my decision, but he had a better understanding of it. I was touched when he said, "I've said this before, but I want to say it again. When you need me I will be here. I'll drop whatever I'm doing if you are in trouble or sick."

Early in the winter of 1988, I decided it was time to give my money away. I was in Michigan visiting my family for the holidays, so I called my new money manager, Glenda Allen. She said to come right over. I drove to a towering building, the National Bank of Detroit, taking with me a copy of the Socially Responsible Investment Directory. When I found Glenda Allen I didn't dawdle. I asked her to dissolve the trust and transfer all the assets directly to a nonprofit organization without paying taxes.

She said that, unfortunately, taxes would be unavoidable because my assets were in an equity trust fund. She made some calculations and told me that I would have capital gains of about roughly $65,000.

I pictured the money sitting in the bank all those years while I ignored it. "All those years of my hard labor, prudent investment, and sweat really earned something!," I thought wryly to myself. I looked at her and said, "Bummer! Well, I want to liquidate everything and give it away, except for what I'll be liable for in taxes. Send $5,000 to me for non-charitable giving and the rest—about $225,000—to a temporary charitable fund I've set up at The Funding Exchange."

Glenda Allen asked me if I would have enough to live on, and I said, "Yes, I guess I'll have to work like everybody else." There were a few more technical details. She needed a few addresses. It was basically very simple.

She was interested in what I was doing. I said, "I'm sorry that our working relationship is so short. Over the years I have been talking to my investment advisers about socially responsible investment, which has been a concern of mine. I edited this *Guide for Socially Responsible Investments*." I gave it to her and she said, "A lot of the guys around here aren't concerned about apartheid or the South Africa issue. I am, and I will read this."

In a funny way, the decision to give away my wealth felt like the first real decision I ever made. It wasn't a rash decision; I had been thinking about it for almost ten years. Yet the choice felt simple. Life presents only a few crystal-clear opportunities to take risks for what you believe and this was one. I've done a lot harder things in my life, and I expect to have to make harder decisions in my future.

*   *   *   *   *

I had considered the idea of putting together my own group to disperse the money, but decided against it. It seemed redundant, since there are a number of good alternative foundations which already do this. It's important to me to support these foundations, and it demonstrates giving up some of my control. I split 50% of the $225,000 among The Funding Exchange's General Fund, the Haymarket People's Fund and the Fund for Southern Communities. I gave another $25,000 to the Peace Development Fund and other intermediaries. I discussed the remaining amount with a few people and gave it to community groups I know from the work I do. I gave to many grassroots social change organizations working for indigenous people's rights, gay rights, anti-intervention work, environmental issues, and anti-racism work. My priority was to give to important projects that have a difficult time getting funding.

*   *   *   *   *

The more I'm "out" and talk openly about my money, the more interesting conversations I have about it. Sometimes I wonder what they're thinking about me that they are not saying. However, what people think isn't something I can control.

After I appeared on the Oprah Winfrey show and after an article I wrote for my alumni magazine came across my father's desk, he wrote me a letter and said, "I think that's about enough publicity for someone who's acting with humility—any more than that and you've definitely crossed the line of self-indulgent demagoguery." He didn't understand that the reason I speak about this publicly is not to call attention to myself, but to make it safer for others to take the leap.

*   *   *   *   *

Since dissolving and giving away the trust, I have felt changes in myself. I spend more time dealing with certain things — like keeping track of how much money is in my bank account, or turning in receipts for reimbursement at work. In the past, I haven't kept careful track of my spending on road trips, and have just subsidized my work place. I would park in a garage to avoid the hassle of looking for parking, and pay for it myself. Now I have to spend time checking things out with other people, operating in a more collective manner. Overall, I think this is good for me.

Living in our simple-living community at the Institute for Community Economics gives me a certain security. However, if I left I wouldn't change my lifestyle. I would look for other people to share my life with in an economical, practical and communal way. Right now ICE pays me enough to cover my housing, utilities and food, and I also have access to a car whenever I need one. Even counting health costs and visits to my family, which ICE pays for, it costs under $8000 a year to support me — and I'm living very well. This gives me a sense of security.

I have great sources of support which give me enough security to let go of my money: good work, community, friends, a support group, and loving relationships. Being part of a larger social movement also increases my sense of security. Perhaps we're only a union of fools trying to build a new society and change our own lives, but I feel inspired and optimistic, knowing that others are doing similar work. Lord knows, I would like to work on behalf of people in Central America, Zaire and the Philippines, but as one person I can only do so much. I feel fortified knowing that I am part of a social movement of people who are doing all this work, and who respect me for doing my piece.

We are all utterly interdependent with other human beings. On some deep level we all realize that, but having money can cover it up. So many of us pay someone to grow our food, build our house, pick up our refuse, educate our children...We even have Third World slaves we never meet, mining our fuel and growing our food at ridiculously low wages. I used to buy services and material comforts, which kept me from relying on the spirit, friends, loved ones, my community. But now I am developing a quality life more interconnected with others, with less dependence on money. I feel that I have a lot to gain, personally and spiritually, from living more simply. I am learning how to give back my privilege for the long-term security and sustainability of the earth. Why should I wait for someone else to take the first step in giving up First World privilege?

JOE AND TERRY HAVENS

Joe, 71, has spent most of his life teaching and practicing psychotherapy. Teresina (or Terry), 81, has worked as a university instructor. For 15 of their 40 years together, they managed a spiritual retreat center in the woods of Western Massachusetts, where they lived in a small wooden cabin without electricity.

Joe: I grew up in an upper-middle-class neighborhood in Kansas City. My father owned a small steel company with 125 employees, but he worried about finances all through the Depression. I remember that he got ulcers trying to meet the payroll.

I studied engineering at MIT and became radicalized through my involvement in the American Student Union, a predecessor of Students for a Democratic Society (SDS). I was a conscientious objector during World War II. After the war I asked myself how to live congruently with my values. I wanted a style of living that would be equivalent in its commitment to the pacifism I experienced during the war. Voluntary poverty was not a very popular lifestyle at the time, but I was drawn to it. So when I was first released from CO camp, I joined Terry and others in the poor Black community of Chester, Pennsylvania.

Terry and I had similar ideals. We were both influenced by Dorothy Day, whom we knew through the Catholic Worker, Charles Gray, Mildred Young (a Quaker who wrote pamphlets on voluntary poverty), John Woolman (another Quaker), Jesus, Gandhi, St. Francis, and Thoreau. Most of these people came out of spiritual traditions.

Terry: As a child, I read a book about Madame Brezhkovska, the "little grandmother of the Russian Revolution." When she was a child she was always giving her coats away to the serfs' children. Her parents would scold her, and she'd say, "Jesus says that if you have two coats you should give one away." St. Francis and Buddha gave their clothes away and wore beggar's clothes. It seemed to me that if you were serious about religion, wearing burlap and gunny sacks was the thing to do!

So (before I met Joe) I joined a voluntary poverty group of Buddhists and Christians in Japan, gave all my clothes away, and turned my traveler's checks over to the community. One of my best experiences in that group was going out on the road with no money, as thousands of other religious seekers have done before. Living on the roadside is a regular part of group life.

All that was before we had children. When we had kids, we lived more middle class, with a good-sized house in Amherst, a car, and trips to the West. Yet we still lived relatively simply compared to some people, and sometimes our children felt deprived.

Joe: Around that time we got some inheritance from Teresina's father, mostly in the form of annuities. We tried to do what he would have wanted for our kids, namely travel and education. We traveled as a family to Japan. I was a little uncomfortable using the money but not uncomfortable enough to do anything about it.

My feelings about class and privilege come from political and spiritual understandings I've developed my whole life. But two powerful experiences of my class privilege stand out. The first was when my son and I were in Morocco. We were on a crowded bus that broke down in the desert. The bus driver said we'd be probably be there overnight, but after a while a truck came along, and an English friend who spoke Arabic yelled, "Can we get on?" The driver kept on moving, but at the same time motioned "jump on." We grabbed our bags and the three of us leaped on. Some of the Moroccans saw what was happening and in an attempt to ride with us, began to run and yell "Stop, stop!" But the driver sped away. He took us because he knew we were foreigners and could pay him, and left the Moroccans because they were poor. There's the privilege, the separation, the barrier.

A second such experience took place in southern Mexico in 1972, when I went to a festival way up in the mountains. I took a tiny, rickety plane to get there, but decided to walk back instead of flying, so I could feel a part of the thousands of local people who went to the festival. I had my Spanish dictionary along so that I could converse, and I enjoyed the others walking with me very much, and they enjoyed me. Then they asked, "How did you get here?" I hesitated and then said, "I came on the little airplane." These were people who were walking many miles to get from their homes to the celebration and back again; some had walked for days. They asked, "How much did that cost you?" I told them. Absolute quiet. I felt their unspoken thoughts: "Look at this man, who can spend 150 pesos to get here," and I felt inside that an enormous gulf had opened between us, because of the difference in privilege. These experiences influenced me a great deal.

When I was 55 my mother died and I inherited $35,000. Terry had her annuity of $10,000 a year, and I had been making a professional salary as a clinical psychologist for 18 years. Still, this inheritance seemed like a lot of money. So I called a special meeting of people whose viewpoints I respected, mostly from our Quaker Friends Meeting, to help me sort out what to do with $20,000 of the inheritance I felt I didn't need. My friends felt it was too small to worry about, that I should keep it in case I needed it, and that I was being a little over-scrupulous. Although we felt they lacked a certain understanding of the political perspective and the ethical concerns Terry and I had, we still listened to them. I put money into loan funds of the Institute for Community Economics instead of giving it away.

Shortly after that we moved to Western Massachusetts, to a cabin in the forest in the Berkshires. It was the abandoned site of a mineral spring resort that had been popular in the 19th century. Here we started a spiritual retreat center which we named Temenos. This was a real change in our lifestyle. We didn't intend to live in such a small cabin with no telephone and no electricity, but there we were and it felt right. It was sort of chosen for us. We have lived there for 15 years.

At Temenos we challenge some of the basic values of society and materialism, both by living so simply and by providing a place for retreats and workshops. Buddhist monks come here regularly on retreat. We've always seen our lifestyle as part of the nonviolent revolution, as part of peacemaking, not as returning to the land or primitivism for its own sake.

Six years ago, a second inheritance landed in our laps — my aunt died leaving me $153,000. It seemed an enormous sum. I felt excitement, but also disbelief and puzzlement — I didn't want to take responsibility for it. By this time, Terry and I were very involved as caretakers of the land at Temenos. I didn't feel that I had the calling or the time to be a philanthropist, and yet, because of my political and economic analysis, I recognized that the money was not mine.

After the indifferent success of the meeting on my first inheritance, I did not call for another special meeting, but instead consulted individually with family and friends about giving away the principal. They did not try to discourage me. After listening to many different kinds of suggestions, I sat down and wrote out my giving criteria and funding areas. The mixture included: projects that sought long-term rather than short-term solutions, Latin America, Third World debt-crisis work, non-violence, spiritual work, and "despair-and- empowerment work" (workshops which help people reach through their numbness about the state of the world to their love for it). I did a lot of research for two years. Both Terry and I believe in a process of discovering truth as we go along and seeing where it leads.

I decided to put $110,000 into three different donor-advised funds—one with the American Friends Service Committee, another with The Funding Exchange, and a third with the Tides Foundation. I don't have the personal burden of the money any more, but I continue making decisions about where to give the principal. Putting the money in these funds, where I can't get it for personal use, feels like it is having my cake and eating it, too: I have no taxes, no ownership, but I can pretty much direct where it goes.

With the AFSC fund, Terry and I began supporting a Third World activist, Father Alamiro, in Brazil. Then we also started supporting two activists in the Lafti Village Development Project, a Gandhian project in India, where we get regular reports from field workers.

I put $20,000 into a zero-interest loan at the Institute for Community Economics (ICE), and later made that into a grant. I invested the final $25,000 or so in Calvert's socially-screened growth fund, but when it grew to $30,000 I again wondered if we should give some of it away. Terry thinks we should keep the $30,000, because it's nice to give money to friends who need it. For example, we recently contributed to a friend's trip to Nicaragua and to another friend's debt-crisis work. But I've been thinking about and struggling with it. I'm still hoping to come up with a group decision-making process; it feels wrong that if I want to do something with the money I don't have to ask anybody. I don't like that kind of arbitrary freedom. I want to spread the responsibility. It's a step toward acknowledging that the money is not our own.

I feel strongly that I don't want tens of thousands of dollars put into keeping us alive. With me at age 71 and Terry at 81, we imagine growing older may bring infirmity and sickness and we don't want this money eaten up by the medical system. We do have Medicare. We want what happens to us to be more like what happens to the average person.

Terry: Our children are worried by our lack of health insurance. We are signing a statement that Joe and I take full responsibility for our health and life, but this does not resolve their feelings.

Before giving away the $110,000, we told our children that we were giving most of it to social change groups and that we planned not to pass any money on to them — just a few special things handed down in the family. Our children did not appreciate our decision. They pointed out the inequity of their children not having the educational and travel opportunities which we all had enjoyed because of the inheritance.

Like it or not, our decisions affect our wider networks, and we need to be mindful of these hidden costs. In our efforts to foster justice in the wider human family, our own family feels hurt. How can we break the chain of inheritance and its underlying social inequity, without causing undue pain at home? I don't know. Yet in some ways giving away my money is only a symbol of giving away privilege — the privilege itself remains. My relatives have money. There's no way to get away from the network of family and friends who have money.

We have a choice about whether or not to have money. People whose babies are starving in Brazil don't have a choice.

Joe: Real security comes from strength of faith and spiritual practice and from a sense of centeredness. Inner security can come only after overcoming fearfulness. We had no significant fears or hesitations about deciding to give our money away. Sure, I had doubts, but not major ones.

Terry: I'm not attached to money very much, but I'm very attached to my paraphernalia: my 2,000-year-old artifacts, ancient tools, a Roman household god my grandfather left me. They are not worth a lot of money, but they mean a lot to me. My security is in my equipment: old files, old papers from courses I'm never going to teach again. I need help getting rid of them. As far as security, I know I can be useful, stimulate and inspire people. No amount of money could buy that.

Joe: That is a beautiful example of inner security. Teresina knows what her capacities are and believes in them. She embodies these values in what she does and in the way she lives. That's security. It's utterly different from financial security. It's the security of satisfaction, knowing one has lived a good life.

*   *   *   *   *

Terry: We don't handle money or financial questions very well. I envy people who just say, "Okay, this is money; we need this amount, so we'll charge these fees," and don't get too involved in it. We make a giant ethical issue of it. We can't even set Temenos conference fees without an outside financial consultant. We're overly attached to money in a negative way. We can't treat it neutrally.

I grew up with a real prejudice against the business world, but I'm changing my attitude. Now I believe that business people are carrying out a lot of important psychological and spiritual innovations, and here we are trying to run Temenos and having a hard time because we don't want to touch money. Disciples of St. Francis didn't believe in touching money, so what did they do? They counted their money with a stick! That's absurd!

I don't think that it was an accident that we inherited this money. Something in the universe decides that if you reject something, it tends to come back and hit you. We have tended to blame and look down on the rich. We felt so superior about not having money that perhaps it was thrown at us so we would have to identify with people who have money and the struggles they go through. We're still struggling with it.

Joe: Different people with a lot of money naturally choose different vocations. As a result of an analysis of the world, some wealthy people appropriately divest themselves of money. That's a very good and very important path. I'd advise people to be conscious, however, about their choice of how much to give away. Don't give your money away on a whim. Be clear and centered about your decision. Another good path for those with money is stewardship. That's a spiritual concept that comes from Christian leadership, and is also practiced by Native peoples who live in balance with the land. A steward has the perspective, "The money is not mine. While I have certain gifts and the responsibility to use the money wisely, I shouldn't have all the power." Whatever our resources are — intelligence, practical skills, creativity, money — stewardship enjoins us to use them for the benefit of the whole society.

BEYOND GUILT AND SHAME

I remember driving through the Bronx as a kid, realizing that something was wrong ... I began to feel acutely responsible for the world and everything I hated that was wrong with it. It seemed like I was at fault for being up near the top of the inequitable system we live in. I felt contempt for the system and for what rich people do and turned that against myself.

— "Elinor Goldfarb"

For many of us, our first response to seeing social injustice is to feel guilty. Guilt is a natural response, a sign we care about others' suffering and recognize something is wrong in the world. For some, the pain of guilt is motivating: Nelia Sargent said it gave her the impetus to take action when she might easily have done nothing; "Sam Murphy" said the guilt he felt about racism motivated his early learning about the causes of injustice.

But for most of us, guilt is not a good motivator. The actions we take based on guilt are forced and heavy and hard to sustain; if our guilt is relieved, the impulse to act fizzles. More often, guilt immobilizes us and makes us feel powerless.

A common way to cope with guilt is to try to suppress it, replacing the pain with numbness. For many of us who are wealthy, this feels better than beating ourselves up — but then we find ourselves acting in strange, "forgetful" ways in relation to our money. Some of us leave checks and letters from the bank or the IRS unopened for weeks or months. We neglect to return calls from the estate or trust manager or from friends who ask about loans. We never take the step to withdraw our investments from companies operating in South Africa and switch them to neighborhood investment.Since to take any constructive action we have to first deal with our guilt and the guilt feels too painful, every step is like slogging through waist-deep glue.

> [For years before and after inheriting money] I tried not to think about it... I thought, "I should be happy! I am one of the lucky people in the world who doesn't have to work for a living. What is the matter with me, why do I feel so bad?" I felt guilty that I had privileges that other people didn't have and I was worthless as a person...
>
> All this time I was getting envelopes from various money things and not opening them. I let them pile up... It was bad at tax time, because I couldn't deal with it—I couldn't face opening those envelopes. So I didn't file my returns and I had a lot of anxiety about the IRS coming after me.
>
> — Betsy Duren

As the result of our denial, our attempts to run from guilt only make us feel worse about ourselves. Even though others may try to reassure us, "Look, you didn't create injustice! It's created by the economic system, and other rich people long ago who had nothing to do with you!" we know that we're benefitting from what is wrong in the world.

Unlike guilt, which stems from feeling bad about our actions (or lack of action), shame stems from feeling bad about who we are. This often makes shame harder to change.

Why would people be ashamed of who they are? Take the example of "Sarah." Her family history included industrialists well known for exploiting their workers during the 19th century in the United States and more recently, for closing many plants in the States and moving them to Third World countries. Even though Sarah and her immediate family now have nothing to do with the company, she grew up feeling ashamed of her name. When meeting new people, she would mumble her name or avoid giving it at all. She tried to hide her money from friends, wore old clothes, and never took people to see her family home. She did her best to deny her money and heritage because she judged herself harshly, and she feared that others would judge her.

Like Sarah, many of us use denial to mask the shame about our wealth and privilege. We practice denial by narrowing our focus, attempting indifference to anyone but ourselves and our immediate family. We deny that we have more than we need, or that there's poverty in the world, or that our actions could make a difference. We even deny that we're wealthy — not hard to do, since it is always possible to find people who are more powerful, more wealthy, and more privileged than we are, or to surround ourselves by people so similar to us that our wealth feels normal.

This denial is further encouraged by the dominant culture. We're taught that the United States is founded on principles of equality and justice, yet the society — already unfairly rich by global standards — constantly reinforces the urge to seek greater and greater wealth. Sociologist Philip Slater calls this "wealth addiction" and describes how the addiction was created by the market economics of corporate America so that more and more consumer goods could be manufactured and bought.

"What distinguishes wealth addicts from other addicts is that they have been largely successful in selling this delusion to the general public," Slater writes. "Wealth addicts have the propaganda machinery of the entire society at their disposal, working full-time to perpetuate their self-deceptions."

Like the suppression of guilt, denial may reduce the anguish of shame but it is an injurious solution. To forever hide who we are, to cut ourselves off from our true caring for the world, and to retreat into numbness has great cost — our sense of integrity and self.

*   *   *   *   *

How can we transcend our guilt and shame? It is a long-term, step-by-step process of bringing our lives into congruence with our values. The goal is not to achieve some ideal purity — say, by giving up all one's wealth tomorrow, or by becoming an ascetic. The goal is to find an honest balance in life, more in accord with the well-known Serenity Prayer:

"God grant me the serenity to accept the things I cannot change, the courage to change the things I can, and the wisdom to know the difference."

Here are some suggestions for dealing constructively with guilt and shame, based on the experiences of the interviewees:

Find support. The first step is to acknowledge and talk about your feelings. Can you identify someone (a friend, lover, or counselor) whom you believe could listen to you without judging, someone who could be an accepting presence as you sort out your feelings? What would it take for you to be able to approach this person?

This step might not be easy. Guilt and shame can be immobilizing, with suppression and denial holding them in place — a self-perpetuating system. You may not only feel bad about what is inside, but also be afraid that others will judge you harshly if they find out. This keeps the guilt and shame bottled up. The only way to break the deadlock is to step out of isolation and start talking. If the first person you try doesn't respond in the ways you need, don't retreat — try someone else.

Pay attention to your values. Talk about your values. What do you believe about the way the world works, the source of your wealth, your responsibility and power? Figure out what your values are — not just what you think you ought to believe, but what really rings true.

Practice self-respect and self-forgiveness. If you uncover some painful differences between what you value and how you live, allow yourself to feel your pain instead of pushing it away. But notice if you turn this pain into self-hatred. Do you secretly believe that hating yourself will motivate you to change? Many people learned this growing up, but actually the opposite is true: self-hatred is immobilizing. The best fertilizer for growth and change is self-acceptance.

Developing self-acceptance takes practice, and it may feel foreign and embarrassing at first. A way to practice is to write down, every day, ten things you appreciate about yourself, no matter how small. Tell them to your confidante. "I pay most of my bills on time." "I am basically a kind human being." You can practice self-forgiveness with the phrase "Even though I _____, I still completely accept myself." (Even though I have way more than other people... even though I have felt paralyzed about my money...) Accepting yourself is not a way to "let yourself off the hook." Rather, it is a way to develop the energy and hope necessary to take sustained action. Appreciate your courage for taking on these difficult issues about your wealth.

Take action. Take steps to bring your life more in accordance with your values. Each step, no matter how small, is worth celebrating. For a while your steps may be about regaining control of your money — opening those neglected envelopes, determining how much you have, how it's managed, and how you will take care of your material needs. You are not looking to exchange guilt and shame about the world for guilt and shame about your own needs. Rather, you are looking for a new sense of balance which values both yourself and others.

After that, your steps may be about discovering what you care about most, and how you can make a difference with your money, time and energy. Changing to socially responsible investments and creating a giving plan; developing a meaningful career instead of living off inheritance; volunteering with a community group; choosing to spend less on luxuries and use the surplus to support work for change — these are a few of many changes that people overcoming their guilt have made over time.

Remember that there is a difference between blaming yourselves for things you did not do (or did before you realized that you had other choices) and taking responsibility for present and future action. You may not be able to change everything overnight, but you can move towards living your values. Pick actions that suit your courage and abilities — not so small that they are token, but not so huge that they're overwhelming.

*   *   *   *   *

Take care of yourself in this process. Change takes persistence and patience. If possible, join with others to think through and act on your next steps. Many people, not just wealthy folks, struggle with how to live closer to their values — support may be more available than you realize! Get appreciation for each step you take, and support to take more steps. Don't give up, but don't add new layers of guilt about what you can't do. Have compassion for yourself, and keep moving.

> You can sit around in your pity pot of guilt and not do anything; that doesn't help anyone, yourself included. Or you can move beyond that stage into action. As soon as I started on that path... I got a hundredfold return.
>
> — Nelia Sargent

REVEALING OURSELVES AS WEALTHY

Every time I hear people say, "People will hurt you somehow if they know you have money," my feeling is, "Not as much as you are hurting yourself."

— Edorah Frazer

Many of us with substantial wealth live in fear that people will find out we have money. We're afraid if our acquaintances and co-workers discover the truth about us, they will lose respect for our work, or see us only as a potential source of money instead of as ourselves, or simply hate and envy us. We often hide the truth even from those we're close to, for fear of losing their friendship.

Why so much fear and secrecy? Wealthy people are envied, admired, and emulated daily across our TV screens and magazine tabloids, and they enjoy privilege and power. But the dominant society's obsession with the rich and famous also promotes many distorted stereotypes about what wealthy people are like. Ask a group of people to complete the phrase, "Rich people are..." and you're likely to get a torrent of adjectives: "Selfish. Shallow. Arrogant. Fake. Uncaring. Condescending. Superficial. Power-hungry." No wonder we're afraid to tell people about our wealth!

Our fears are sharpened by the grains of truth they hold. There are reasons for many people to be distrustful of and angry at rich people — not as individuals, but as a class. We live in a society in which a small number of individuals and families control a disproportionate share of wealth and power — and conspire, more or less consciously, to maintain and extend this wealth and power through a host of cultural, economic, legal and social means. Regardless of our individual personalities or choices or values, we are, by virtue of being wealthy, symbols of power and apparent representatives of a system that harms the life of many, many people.

The stereotypes that we face and fear are fueled by a powerful myth in U.S. society. This myth says people become wealthy because they are smart or lucky or ruthless enough to clamber to the top where they can enjoy the good life as reward for their struggle. This myth is trumpeted and reinforced daily across our TV screens and magazines. Inundated with these "success stories," most people stop seeing the system and instead focus on hating and envying those individuals who symbolize the wealth. People may be aware their stereotypes of rich people are exaggerations, but their emotions — anger, resentment, and judgment — are real and can hit us hard and personally.

With the threat of such rejection hanging over us, it's no wonder many of us choose to associate only with people of our own class. It's certainly more comfortable! But many of us seeking to make a better world are deliberately involved with a wide range of people working to change injustice. It may be especially hard for us to be open about our money, because people who care about justice often view the rich as "the enemy," the source of the social problems. If we reveal our wealth, won't we be mistrusted politically? Our co-workers live off meager activist salaries — won't they resent our surplus? Our social change organizations struggle daily for money — won't we be expected to use our wealth to bolster the shortfalls of the budget? If we work as fundraisers for political causes, won't our effectiveness be jeopardized if we disclose our own wealth? For all these reasons and more, we keep secret.

> I worked as an assistant to someone at the League of Women Voters whom I admired very much. Even though I worked closely with her for seven years, I never told her about my money. I lived in dread that she would find out. I wanted to be "Penny Lippincott," the community activist and not "Penny Lippincott," the philanthropist. I wanted to be a worker, an equal.
>
> — "Penny Lippincott"

Although hiding our wealth protects us from people's judgments, as with most secrets it has costs. On the personal level, we often feel fake. We're reluctant to get too close; the wall of protection we've built keeps us lonely and isolated. We live in fear of being found out.

And what a barrier it creates in accomplishing the changes we want for the world! The stereotypes about rich people continue, to the detriment of everyone. Many poor and working-class people would feel energized and inspired if they knew people with substantial resources were working with them for social change, and many more wealthy people might contribute their hearts and talents to bettering the world if they felt welcomed and understood as who they are. Just as there are stereotypes of poor people as lazy and destructive, and of middle-class people as apathetic, stereotypes of wealthy people obscure our seeing people different from ourselves as human beings and reaching out to them. All these class stereotypes keep us distrusting each other, instead of working together to change the systems of injustice which hurt us all and threaten all of our survival.

Talking about our wealth is not easy, especially since this dominant society has strong taboos against financial disclosure. (It is far more common to hear the intimate details of people's sex lives than to learn what their income is.) The extent of our openness varies all the way from those who have disclosed they have inherited wealth with a few close friends after years of building trust, to those of us who speak about being wealthy philanthropists on national talk shows. And although some of us have had difficult experiences — strained relationships, repeated unwanted requests for money — the surprising and heartening truth is that, for the most part, becoming more honest about who we are has brought us immense relief, release from pretense, a deeper sense of integrity, and more genuine relationships.

Here is one wealthy activist's experience at a conference for progressive cultural workers:

> People were talking about arts funding in communities, and about the power of the ruling class — the ruling class this and the ruling class that. I said to myself, "They're playing my song! They're talking about me, but they don't understand my people." I knew that seeing us as inhuman was not helping them, and I could do something about it. But I was terrified. I dealt with my fear as deeply and rapidly as I could, and finally I raised my hand. At the microphone I said, "I am a rich person. I do a lot of work with rich people. There are rich people who, in our lifetime, will never be reached by the social change movement, and there are a bunch of us who are already completely active in it. There are also a lot of people in between who are potentially reachable, but are very confused and scared — terrified, in fact." ... By the end of the day I had gotten so many positive responses, I realized what I had done: I had made it safe to *be myself* in that community.

If you are someone who has been afraid and would like to become more open about your money, here are a few tips from some of us who have taken the plunge:

Talk with other wealthy people first. Many people have found it liberating to begin by attending conferences of wealthy people and trying out disclosure there. (See Funding Exchange and Threshold Foundation in the resource list.)

Build your own self-respect. Difficulties about disclosing wealth often have as much to do with your self-image as they do with how others might view you. The better you feel about who you are, the more you can put others' judgments into perspective.

Start slowly and be selective. Use your discretion about what to say, when and to whom. In many relationships, revealing our financial situation is not important for honest closeness, but in others it is. Start where it is important, with one person whom you trust, at a safe time to really talk about it.

Be yourself, vulnerable and "ordinary." You might explain why you want this person to know about your money. Be open about your fear. Since wealthy people often use their money to keep people at bay (out of fear, disdain for poorer people, pain from past encounters, shame), make it clear your intent is to be more honest.

Be prepared for reactions; be prepared to listen. Many people do have strong feelings about wealth. If the person you disclose to has strong reactions, try not to be defensive. If you can, explore what's underneath their reactions by listening empathetically and asking more about what they feel and why — not to "fix it" and take away the discomforts, but to understand each other better. Remember that the point is building the relationship; their reactions are valuable information about them, *not true reflections on you.*

Some examples:

Reaction: "Oh, so you're rich. I always thought you were different, even arrogant.

Possible Reply: "I'm just me—no better or worse than you. I'd like to hear about what you see as different about me; what do you want me to change?"

Reaction: "Wow, you have *that* much! Gee, that means your annual income has to be around $xxx,xxx! Well, I guess you don't need the salary this organization pays you."

Possible Reply: True, I don't need it to survive, but I really value earning my way here like everyone else. What else does it mean to you, to know I have this money?"

Develop policies about giving. Many people keep their money secret because they're afraid of being asked for money, by friends, organizations, and even strangers. Rather than dealing with this issue through hiding, you can develop clear policies about your giving that enable you to respond to requests openly and humanly. You can learn to say "no" in a graceful manner that honors your relationships. With these skills, you can be much more relaxed and open about your situation. Here are some examples of giving policies:

I'm glad to consider your request, but I don't make decisions on the spot. If you'll please write down what you're asking for and why, I'll think about it and discuss it with you more in a few days.

Mostly, I give only to foundations which fund the work I support. I give just a few contributions each year to individuals, usually people whose work I know quite well.

Yes, I do occasionally lend money. My policy is to lend no more than $2,000 at a time, for no more than 18 months. I would want to work out a written agreement with you, including an interest rate and a schedule of payments.

(For more information, see *Economics As If the Earth Really Mattered*, and *The Challenges of Wealth*, listed in the bibliography.)

Keep taking the next step. If you have a bad experience, talk it over with someone you trust and see what you can learn. Try again. Celebrate your successes. There may be certain people you choose never to tell. That's fine; there's no rule. The point is to have these decisions come from reasoned choice, not automatic fear. Remember that creating more and more places where you are fully yourself is worth a bit of work. And if you are someone committed to building a better world, remember that revealing yourself as wealthy is not only breaking your own isolation but also helping to change the forces that hold class oppression in place.

FAMILIES AND MONEY

Money in some families is more powerful than blood.

— Ram Dass

Giving away large amounts of money is a decision that can arouse strong reactions from the people we love. Those of us drawn to give our resources often wonder how to discuss our decision-making with our families, partners and children. What kinds of family issues confronted the people whose stories are told here? What lessons can be passed on?

Most of us were working on coming to terms with our upbringing long before we considered giving away wealth. Before we could even begin to question family norms about money, we needed to become more aware of our past. What spoken and unspoken attitudes about money did we inherit from our families? Which of those values did we want to keep? Which did we want to discard? Sorting through these questions was an essential part of our becoming adults, as it is for young people of any class background.

Many of us who receive wealth from our families need to "cut the strings" attached to the money. Often the strings are emotional rather than concrete: "Remember, this wealth has been in the family since your great-grandfather built his business from nothing. Make him proud by increasing it before you pass it on to the next generation of our family." Even if this message is never said aloud, we often feel the pressure of family expectations. Sometimes the strings on our money are legal. Families sometimes set up trusts which dictate when we could touch the principal until some arbitrary point when we would magically become capable of mature decision-making.

"Cutting the strings" can mean going to court to break these trusts or working to influence how the trust principal is invested, or negotiating to prevent future restrictive trusts.

Even when no strings are intended, our ability to make decisions about our money is often confused by our relationships with those who have given it to us. What do we feel towards them? — love? resentment? longing? Does the money feel like a replacement for closeness? Do we feel it cheapened otherwise important relationships by casting them in monetary terms? If our "good fortune" was because of a death, our feelings are often even more complex: appreciation mixed with grief, guilt for being happy about the money, anger at issues unresolved in the relationship. All these family ties make it hard to think clearly about the money in our lives, and complicate any consideration of giving it away.

Love and money are too often entangled in our families. Sometimes the things money can buy are used as substitutes for affection. If our families could only experience "togetherness" by spending money together on vacations, fancy presents, shopping, dining, the country club or travel, money became a symbol of and vehicle for connection. And if we questioned our family values about money, it was often interpreted as rejection.

Wealthy women carry additional burdens. With rare exceptions, we are not trained to deal with money nor given any information about family finances. Some of us were actively prevented from finding out how much money we had, or from getting control over it. Unlike the men in our families, we are not expected to know the difference between a stock and a bond, let alone participate in important decisions about family investments. Our stock brokers and trust officers treat our questions with patronizing disdain. It often takes us years to overcome our feelings of inadequacy and humiliation enough to take charge of our finances.

*   *   *   *   *

Healing from our family's emotional heritage is an essential step in the process of deciding how to use our money. This healing and separating process often requires us to create distance between ourselves and our family. But as we feel stronger, we can often restore or create more positive relations with our families, even if we take actions which trigger their disapproval.

If you are someone considering giving a lot, and you're wondering about ways to minimize estrangement from your family, here's what we can offer you based on our experiences:

Rediscover pride in your family. Find the aspects of your family history and heritage you can openly be proud of and share them with your family. Appreciate whatever advantages you are thankful for, like education, travel, or other things given to you by your parents. This can help provide a positive base of connection when taking other steps.

Take small steps to build trust. If you have never been able to communicate well with family members, work to build connections before delving into divisive money matters. You might invite a family member to do something social with you, like go to lunch or attend a concert. When you are together, concentrate on what you enjoy about this person, not on your differences. Another small step might involve asking family members to join you in contributing to a specific cause you imagine they could support.

Share who you are. Talk about your social change perspective in a way that is easy to understand. Tell how your thinking developed, and why you care about the things you do. Explain that you are sharing your beliefs, not to criticize anyone, but because your values are important to you and you want the family to know you better. Your family may be better able to understand your actions if they have this context — even if they end up disagreeing with you.

Ask for help. Let family members know that you are actively thinking about money issues — what to do with assets, how to invest responsibly, whether and how to give away large amounts. If it is clear that you are thinking carefully about your material needs and those who might depend on you, some of their worries may dissolve. Genuinely asking for help, making it clear that you value their opinions while you may not follow their advice, can be a way to build mutual respect.

Listen to their concerns. With creativity, you may be able to lessen their worries without compromising your values. (For instance, fears about your long-term security might be muted by buying ample insurance.) Even if you do nothing to address your family members' concerns, giving them a chance to offer advice and listening non-defensively will probably help the relationship.

Give reassurance. If you love them, tell them so. Let them know that your actions are not intended as a judgment of them. You are not rejecting them — even if you no longer spend money in the same ways. If money alters your ability to take part in family activities, find ways to engage them in activities that do not require much money. In whatever ways you can, express your genuine appreciation.

*   *   *   *   *

Giving away assets affects not only our families, but all of our loved ones. How easy or hard this is depends on the degree of harmony and shared values that exists in our relationships.

All couples, whatever their financial status, have to work through differences in order to create a workable pattern of earning, spending, saving, and giving. When one person in the relationship has large amounts of assets and the other has little, this can present dizzying complications. Most of our partners (though not all) strongly support our wish to contribute substantially to social change. Even so, we need to do lots of talking about how much, when, and in what ways it would affect us as a couple or family. Based on our experiences, here are some suggestions of ways to work with your partner as you navigate this decision-making:

Identify and talk about values. Some couples have dealt only indirectly with differences in values, attitudes, and practices about money, so conflicts emerge each time a new question comes up. If this is true for you, try setting aside some specific time for you and your partner to talk directly about your underlying differences in relation to money. Share information about how your experiences growing up affect your current attitudes. Once experiences and values are out in the open, it may be easier to make decisions and take action together.

Provide information. What exactly are your assets? How are they invested? How much are you considering giving and to what? Sometimes partners feel anxious from simply not knowing. Even a partner who is not involved directly in decisions about money can benefit from a more complete financial picture.

Invite your partner to be involved in financial decisions that will affect your life together. When a partner is left out of these decisions, she or he may feel disempowered and vulnerable. While some partners may not want to be involved, the chance to refuse participation can itself be important.

*   *   *   *   *

When children are involved, the decision to give away substantial assets means thinking carefully about the issue of inheritance.

The dominant society offers such inadequate safety nets that most families want to leave their children some amount of money to help them along. In families that have been wealthy for generations, the norm of passing fortune on from parents to children is so powerful that people rarely question whether inheritance is in their family's best interest. Even so, many of us decide to leave our children substantially less than we ourselves received, because we believe that a large inheritance will not add to our children's well-being. After all, inheriting large amounts of money early in life can be debilitating. One wealthy man we know described coming into money in this light:

> I had just graduated from college and spent three months in Europe, using up the last money in my bank account. Then I returned home and got the first money from the inheritance. This was really bad for my personal motivation... The money made it possible for me to get hung up on the question of 'What's the perfect thing for somebody with my privilege and ability to choose to do?' and never feel satisfied.

A common compromise is to pass on enough to enable our children to get through college, but not so much that they won't have to work for a living. Limiting their inheritance in this way leaves more resources available for the funding of social change — thereby investing in a world our children and others of their generation would find good to live in.

Every family must create its own norms about money. For what they are worth, we offer some guidelines to consider based on our own values about money, children, and inheritance:

Make open discussion about money a regular part of family life. Plan explicit education for both girls and boys about financial issues and management, at levels appropriate to each stage of their development. Provide easier tasks and decisions for young children (such as making spending decisions and keeping a banking account), and add more complex ones as they grow older.

Help your children find their work. Encourage and support young people to discover what most interests them and to pursue a way to earn their own living.

Clearly distinguish love from money. Make it clear that however much (or little) money you leave them, you love your children deeply and are available to help them if they need you. Help children separate feelings about family money from love and appreciation of family members.

Give without strings. If you do give your children wealth, provide them with the power to decide for themselves what to do with it, offering guidance only as they want it.

*   *   *   *   *

We don't mean to imply that it will be easy to resolve family issues about money. Sometimes differences are intractable: Charles Gray's 31-year marriage ended over his choice of lifestyle; Tracy Gary had to take her mother to court before she won control over her own assets. But we know of other families who, while not thrilled with the decision of their family member to give away principal, stayed close and supportive throughout the process. Often such decisions did cause tensions, but with honest communication and the passage of time, rifts healed and the people involved reconnected with renewed respect. Two years after his dad accused him of being a Marxist revolutionary, Chuck Collins's father shed tears of pride at a ceremony in which Chuck received an award for community service which highlighted the unusual extent of his financial contributions. When we take the leap to live our lives with internal integrity, we open the door to more genuine, though not necessarily more peaceful, relationships with all our loved ones.

> My father wouldn't agree, but I see my family as all of humanity. I do not feel I am giving my money away outside my family to distant causes. I feel I am simply sharing what I have *with* my larger family.
>
> — "Rob Stoner"

FINDING MEANINGFUL WORK

If the world were merely seductive, that would be easy.
If it were merely challenging, that would be no problem.
But I arise in the morning torn
      between a desire to improve the world,
And a desire to enjoy the world
This makes it hard to plan the day.

— E.B. White

Wealthy people, especially those of us who inherit large sums before we've chosen an occupation, face some particular dilemmas about our life's work. On one hand, we long for meaningful work as a channel for our creative energies and as a way to contribute to society. Performing a productive role is a basic human need, as important as food or love, a vehicle for self-esteem, personal identity and social recognition.

On the other hand, we look around and see that most people are trapped in jobs that are either numbingly dull, degrading or dangerous. Many people cannot find jobs, and others, such as artists, social change activists, and people who are parenting, perform important work for which they are unpaid or poorly paid. No wonder most people dream of striking it rich so they can stay home and take it easy!

Most societies do not guarantee worthwhile work, just as they do not provide for other basic human needs such as decent, affordable housing or adequate health care. In an ideal world, all human beings would be encouraged to discover their true calling and to perform a share of the work needed to support the community. But under present conditions, it is very difficult for most people to do socially beneficial and personally fulfilling work — even for the wealthy, who are privileged to have many more choices about their work.

Many of us who inherit money as young adults especially struggle with work. Some of us torment ourselves by searching for the perfect job, using our money to drift from one half-hearted occupation to another, never making a commitment, never "growing up." Others feel intense pressures (spoken or unspoken) from our families to enter high-status professions — whether or not the profession is personally fulfilling — because wealthy people are supposed to perpetuate their privilege in that way.

Those of us who want our life's energy to help create a more just and peaceful world, face all these dilemmas, plus others. Jobs to change the world are scarce and poorly paid compared to most professions, and by and large, neither our families nor society at large give the work status or recognition. Unlike becoming a doctor or a lawyer, there is no recognized, accredited "career path" for social change work. And because resources for social change work are so scarce, it is easy to feel guilty about accepting some of those resources as our pay. Should we give our money away and get a well-paid job? Should we create great social change work and fund it ourselves? What are the options and how do we decide?

Here are four distinct choices concerning work. If you are someone with money who wants to make ethically conscious work choices, we hope this will help you sort through some of the possibilities. Your ultimate choice may incorporate aspects of each alternative, or you might craft a path that starts with one option and later moves you to another.

Find a fulfilling career. Perhaps you want "a regular job" — because you need it to feel good about yourself, or because living off inherited money feels ethically wrong, or because you are attracted to a line of work in which satisfying jobs are available. Several people featured in this book chose this path: Edorah Frazer, because she felt her true calling was as a teacher; Joseph Collins of the Institute for Food and Development, because he enjoyed his career as a researcher and educator and didn't want his life centered around his money; Chuck Collins of the Institute for Community Economics, because living off inheritance felt wrong and he was able to find paid and fulfilling social change work.

If this path appeals to you there are still several issues to think through.

Do you need schooling, and if so, will you use your own money to fund your education? Several of the interviewees did, subsequently giving large parts of their assets to fund social change once their work was established.

What lifestyle feels right? Many people whose stories are included here — Nelia Sargent, Joe and Terry Havens, Betsy Duren — made a choice to "live simply" and derive their security and satisfaction from community, good work, and nature rather than from material goods. This enabled them to do social change work for little pay and use most of their assets for progressive change. (See *Living More with Less* in the bibliography.) Other givers wanted to enjoy a higher level of material comfort, and so kept substantial assets ($100,000 – $1 million or more) to supplement their earnings before giving away the rest.

Fund your own work. Perhaps the work you want to do doesn't exist as a paying job, or you feel it's ethically wrong to "take a job from someone who needs it" when you don't need the money, or you want more freedom or meaning in your work than a regular job could give. In this case, you might decide to live on investment income or assets while you do the work of your choice, as John Steiner, Sallie Bingham, and Tracy Gary did. Here are some of the issues involved:

How will you be held accountable for the quality of your work? Even if you know you are completely dependable, many organizations will take you more seriously if you fit into a structure of organizational accountability. If you decide to volunteer with an organization, you can request that they supervise you as they would a regular employee, since this is your main work and not a sideline. If you decide to work independently or to start your own organization, you might organize a small group of people to be your "board" and meet with you periodically. This board can listen to your progress and difficulties, help you make responsible decisions, and make sure you're on track in relation to your goals.

Will you feel good about yourself, using the money to support yourself? In order for this choice to work, you have to make peace with yourself about using privilege in this way, when so few people can exercise this option; you have to be comfortable with people knowing you have money; and you need to feel fine without the social validation provided by a regular pay check.

Some people feel more at ease with this choice if they live simply. This way, they can use most of their assets to fund social change, while using no more resources to support themselves than anyone else would doing the same work. (See The New Road Map Foundation's work on "Financial Independence" in the bibliography.) Others make peace with this option by using the privilege to "leverage" benefits for others as they support themselves. For instance, someone who wants to work as an artist — traditionally a difficult way to earn a living — might use an inheritance to support herself in that work, while at the same time setting up studio space and securing funding for other artists.

Make philanthropy your work. Perhaps you enjoy working with money, and are excited about the impact you can have funding social change work. Then, like Sally Bingham, George Pillsbury, and Ram Dass, you could make philanthropy part of your life's work. Some questions to consider include:

Do you want to set up a foundation or charitable trust? If you are certain you want to contribute significant amounts of money over time, there can be substantial tax benefits to setting up a charitable legal entity. (See appendix, "Tax-Wise Charitable Giving.")

Would you enjoy a job with an existing foundation? The National Network of Grantmakers is a network of over 200 grant-making organizations that support progressive change, and many of its member groups have staff positions. You can also volunteer to serve on the board of certain foundations.

Should you be making funding decisions alone? There are good reasons to question the wisdom of such an approach. (See Chapter on "Sharing Power and Privilege.") You might want to pool money with others (see A Territory Resource and the Network for Social Change in the Resource List), or pull together a group of people you respect to help you make decisions, or give through an existing foundation, especially one where granting decisions are made by community activists (see The Funding Exchange in the Resource List.)

Do you want to manage your own investments as well as give money away? Money management can be a full-time job. How your money is invested can contribute to social change on its own merits — for instance, if it is providing venture capital for new experiments in responsible business, or supporting established socially useful businesses, or providing low-interest loans for low-income communities building their economic self-sufficiency. (In the resource list, see the Social Ventures Network, the National Network of Community Loan Funds, and the Industrial Cooperative Association.)

Become a "social entrepreneur." The term "entrepreneur" often means someone who starts a business, aiming to make lots of money. Social entrepreneurs also start businesses, but their aims are somewhat different. If they make their money in traditional forms of business (not necessarily improving the world), they then use their money and influence for social purposes. For instance, Phil Villers decided as a young man that the best way he could contribute to the world was to make a lot of money, so he started several computer companies. Eventually he set up a foundation with $40 million. Ben Cohen did not expect to make a fortune with his ice cream business, but the company's amazing success enabled him to capitalize the Ben and Jerry's Foundation and to use his substantial influence organizing businesses to support social change.

Other social entrepreneurs start organizations with the express purpose of furthering social change. For instance, Tracy Gary used her money, skill and passion to start The Women's Foundation. Businesses like Seventh Generation (marketing environmentally helpful products) and Rainforest Crunch (working to save our endangered rainforests) are not ashamed to make a profit, but the money is secondary to the company's mission.

If you are drawn to this option, here are some issues to consider:

If your aim is to make a lot of money, what is your motivation? Do you need to make lots of money to feel good about yourself, because such "success" is socially validated? Are you rationalizing your desire for money by saying you'll later use it for social good?

What are your ethical boundaries and how will you remain accountable to your ethics? Many ways of making large sums of money, through investments or business, are profitable because they are part of an unfair or unhealthy economic system. For instance, lots of money can sometimes be made in real estate speculation, while hurting many low-income residents through neighborhood gentrification. Do the ends justify the means? To what degree? What are your ethical boundaries? For many people, even those of us with a strong social conscience, the more money we have the more we spend on ourselves. Larger and larger sums just start to feel "normal" to us and our associates. For help with all these issues, you might want to organize a "board" of friends and colleagues whose values and lifestyles you respect to regularly give you feedback and perspective about your choices.

What if you don't make money, or if you lose the money you have? Trying to get rich can be a risky business. You might do best if you share Ben Cohen's attitude:

> In starting this business, I never expected to make a lot of money. That was never our goal, and whenever we took a risk or had a decision to make, we always said, "What do we have to lose?" And the answer was, "Nothing." If I lost or gave away so much money I didn't have much left, it wouldn't be so bad. I mean, I can always go get a job. And that is the worst thing that could happen. We would be back where we were before Ben & Jerry's started. And you know, that wasn't such a bad place to be.

These four alternatives are only meant as guidelines as you construct your work in the world. You might mix and match aspects of the various options, or move from one choice to another over time, or invest your own. There are many "right" choices. Even if you never put to rest all of the ethical dilemmas posed by the issues of work, we hope you'll find it exciting to craft your work path consciously, and to pursue that path with creativity and determination.

BEN COHEN

Ben and his friend Jerry Greenfield founded the Ben & Jerry's ice cream company, based in Vermont. By 1987, the company had grown from a tiny shop in an abandoned gas station to the third largest superpremium ice cream company in the United States.

My family started out lower-middle class and ended up upper-middle class. My mother was a housewife, and my father worked for the post office and later as an accountant for the state.

As a kid, I learned about the history of the Jewish people. That history was essentially one of oppression: usually Jews were treated as second-class citizens, scapegoats, and, at times, slaughtered. I saw parallels with Black people, who are also treated as second-class citizens.

I was taught that all people are equal and that we should try to help those less fortunate than ourselves. At the same time, I learned that we were supposed to hate people who lived in other countries and we were supposed to want to blow them up because they lived on the other side of some imaginary line. I had a real problem accepting that.

I didn't graduate from college. I worked as a taxicab driver, a night mopper, a Pinkerton guard, a short order cook, an assistant superintendent of an apartment building, a Yellow Pages deliverer, and a garbage man. I lived in the slums of New York City and Chicago for a while, and I certainly saw how the other half lives. Before we started Ben & Jerry's, I was teaching pottery and crafts at a school for emotionally disturbed kids. Not the traditional MBA route into business!

When our shop first opened in 1978 in a renovated gas station in Burlington, Jerry was in charge of making the ice cream, and I was in charge of scooping it and making crepes. When the wholesale division got going, Jerry took charge of making ice cream in our plant, and I took charge of sales and marketing. Now that the business has grown so much, I'm away a lot, travelling about a third of the time. I give talks, and work with other businesses becoming more socially responsible. I also work for the group One Percent for Peace, whose goal is to redirect 1% of the military budget to a positive peace agenda — through building bonds of friendship among nations and meeting basic human needs in the U.S. and around the world. I was one of its founding members. When my friend Jeff Furman originally presented the idea to me, I said, "Boy, this idea sounds really marketable! I think it would be easy for people in the general population to say, 'Let's take 1% of the money that we're already paying into the military budget, and just redirect it so we're using it to make friends instead of building walls of fear.'" Jeff mentioned it to a few other people, and we held a meeting of about 40 to 50 people, and started organizing from there. I was the interim executive director. Now that we've hired a full-time executive director, I'm a member of the board and of the steering committee.

It's only since I've gotten involved in business and started to play around with numbers in the millions that I have begun to gain even a vague sense of how much a billion dollars is. Forty percent of the country's budget goes to the military — $300 billion a year. Did you know that 30,000 children die each day of hunger and preventable diseases? If the money spent stockpiling weapons were redirected to meeting human needs, it would change the world.

One percent of Ben and Jerry's net profits are going to One Percent for Peace, but more importantly, we have developed an ice cream novelty called the Peace Pop. Through the Pop we generate public support for One Percent for Peace by endorsing it and spreading information on our package. That advertising space is worth a hell of a lot more money than 1% of our pre-tax profits will ever be. One Percent for Peace is essentially a marketing project. First we'll sell the idea to the grassroots, and once that's accomplished we'll try to push it through Congress. [1]

My major contribution to the community is influencing Ben & Jerry's to be more socially responsible. It involves a lot more than giving away some of our pre-tax profits. That's a small part of our general social responsibility. From early on we've had free ice cream give-aways, free movie festivals, and other cultural festivals.

Ben & Jerry's held a voter registration drive in retail shops in the state of Vermont. It didn't involve any significant money, but felt like a major contribution to the community. We registered over 1,000 voters, a lot for such a small state. Imagine if you did that at all retail shops around the country! People go to places of business, but we don't register them there; we make them go to inconvenient places during working hours.

For our brownie ice cream sandwiches we're starting to use a bakery run by a Buddhist group in Yonkers. This group provides for homeless people and teaches them how to become bakers. So we're doing business with a supplier whose profits are going entirely into the community. We're working on finding more suppliers like that.

I've come up with a lot of these ideas, but we're starting to encourage people within the company to think along similar lines and generate their own ideas.

Here was one creative idea: instead of spending marketing money on TV, radio and newspaper, we wanted to adopt a subway station in New York City. We went as far as picking the stop at Broadway and 72nd street, a transfer point for a lot of people from different economic groups. Fixing up this subway stop, unlike advertising, would directly improve the quality of life for people in the city. Unfortunately, the city never let us do it.

Traditionally, the bottom line of most businesses has been measured solely in terms of how many dollars are left over at the end of the year. Therefore, every decision that a business makes is based on what is going to make the most money. At Ben & Jerry's, we've redefined the bottom line. We've said that our bottom line consists of two equal parts. One is making a reasonable profit for shareholders, and the other is helping to improve the quality of life for the members of our communities and for all people. If we fail in either one of these areas, we have failed as a business. We're trying to integrate a concern for the community into all of our business decisions. The Peace Pop is a good example. It's a high-quality product, it makes a profit, and it seeks to generate popular support to redirect the resources of our country to help improve the quality of life for all people.

It's important for the business to be public about what it's doing, because if you do something that's designed to help a problem but nobody knows about it, then it can't influence or educate other people. Ben & Jerry's represents .000001% of the national business wealth — a tiny speck. We do our little bit — which is more than most other businesses do — but in terms of solving social problems, we can't do much until a lot of other people pick up the idea.

We meet with other business people. We're part of the Social Ventures Network, and I'm also working with the newly formed Progressive Business Association, which is an alternative to the Chamber of Commerce and embodies the kind of values we're talking about. I speak at a lot of colleges and universities and find that MBA students are very receptive. I'm putting together a two-day workshop with a few other cutting-edge businesses, like Patagonia, which gives 10% of its profits to environmental causes. The workshops will teach values, and hopefully transform people's thinking so that they make their businesses more socially responsible.

Ben and Jerry's is part of several communities: the first is our company, the people who work here. The second is the local community. Then there's the national community and the world. There's always a dynamic tension in balancing the needs of those different communities.

At times in the history of the company, employees have felt that we give too much to the outer communities and not enough to them. When that happens, we look at the issues and make adjustments. For instance, five years ago our plant was makeshift, overcrowded, and didn't have an employee break room or any other amenities. Pay was low, benefits were lower, and yet we were giving money to the community. People felt they were not being taken care of. So as the company grew and had more money, we put more of it into the "family." Wages and benefits went up, the quality of the working environment improved, and we're now in a modern, state-of-the-art ice cream plant. Jerry started the "Joy Committee," a committee based on infusing more joy into the experience of working here. Workers do their committee work on salaried time. This past year we've been going through an organizational development process with an outside consultant, instituting a more participatory management system. We're trying to get employee input and involvement in all areas of the organization.

We have a seven-to-one salary ratio, where the highest-paid person in our company is not paid any more than seven times what the lowest person gets. In traditional businesses, the salary ratio is often 200-1. We're trying to close that gap. It gives the higher-paid people an incentive to pay the lower-paid people more, so they can increase their salary, too. I get about $100,000 a year, which is at the highest end. The lowest is about $16,000.

When we first went public and sold company stock on the market, we gave some stock to our employees. The second time, employees had an opportunity to buy it at a lower price, and now there's an employee stock ownership program. I think employee ownership is great.

The whole concept of becoming a publicly-held company was to share the wealth. Originally we sold our stock just within the state of Vermont because we wanted our community to be the owners of the business. That way, as the business prospered, the community that supported us would also prosper. We set a very low minimum price for the stock — for $126 you could become a shareholder in Ben & Jerry's — and we advertised it to the mainstream Vermont community, not to the financial community. We had ads in the first section of the newspaper, the one with the clothing ads. We also travelled around the state and held meetings to make it truly available to everyone. Over time, one out of every hundred people in Vermont became stockholders. I always felt like we were holding the business in trust for the community. After all, the community allows you to exist. People in the community buy your product. They provide the infrastructure; they provide all the resources that you use; they provide everything except the idea.

Once the business was doing well, we decided that the company would give away $7\frac{1}{2}$% of its pre-tax profits. I felt that the best vehicle would be through a foundation independent of the company. So, in 1986, we started the Ben and Jerry's Foundation. To get it launched I gave it about $500,000 of my personal stock. The Foundation sold that stock in the initial public stock offer ing, got the cash, and used it as its initial endowment.

When I gave the stock to set up the Ben and Jerry's Foundation, I sold another $500,000 worth of stock to use myself. I figured I'd go one to one. I wouldn't feel okay about taking out $500,000 for myself unless I was giving $500,000 away. I still think in terms of this one-to-one ratio, and whenever I spend another bunch of money on myself, I plan to keep that ratio the same.

I've got more money than I can use in many lifetimes, and I'm still giving gobs of it away. I just don't need that much. I would much rather use it to exert influence and to help people meet their basic needs, than to buy lots of luxuries. My lifestyle is not much different from what it was before I made all this money.

The one change is that I bought a house a year ago, the first house I've owned. It was a big thing for me. I really like it. I have some middle-of-the road furniture, and that's about what I own. My car is owned by the business. My office isn't particularly lavish and I like it. I'm choosing a lifestyle I feel comfortable with, that I do not feel guilty about. I would not feel comfortable spending money on myself while other people are starving and dying. A child's life half-way around the world is as important and valuable as a child's life three blocks away from here.

I never expected to make a lot of money starting this business. That was never our goal, and whenever we took a risk or had to make a decision, we always said, "What do we have to lose?" and the answer was, "Nothing." If I lost or gave away so much money I didn't have much left, it wouldn't be so bad — I mean, I can always go get a job. And that's the worst thing that it'd be. We would be where we were before Ben & Jerry's started. And, you know, that wasn't such a bad place to be.

1. To learn more about this effort, contact One Percent for Peace, P.O. Box 658, Ithaca, N.Y. 14851, 607/272-1919.

JOHN STEINER

For several key years of the peace movement, John's one-on-one funding helped many vital projects get off the ground. He now consults with businesses and non-profits and is raising a family.

As a young man, my father went into business with his brothers manufacturing toys. The company, Kenner Toys, became one of the most successful of its kind in the country.

I was an only child raised in a Jewish family. We lived an upper middle class existence and never wanted for money. I went to a summer camp, where I formed many of my values: the importance of sharing and giving, and taking care of other people. My parents taught me a lot about valuing other people — my mother is a social worker, and father has always been very generous, warm and concerned.

In 1966 my father and his brothers sold Kenner to General Mills, and my father passed some of the money on to me. I went to Harvard, and after graduating went to Venezuela through a community development organization called ACCION International. When I got back to the United States, I went through a prolonged identity crisis — it took me 15 years to get my act together. If I'd been forced to earn a living during those years, perhaps my identity crisis would have been shorter; then again, maybe I would have ended up in jail or in a mental hospital!

For three years I did psychoanalysis and lived at a Zen Center. Since it was the 1960s, I watched a lot of people get involved with social action, but I wasn't together enough to do much work in the world. The one issue that stayed with me during my years at the Zen Center was the madness between the United States and the Soviet Union, the reality that both countries continued to build nuclear bombs. I would think about this during meditation. When you meditate you're supposed to watch your thoughts and feelings come and go, but that thought about the bombs did not go. It stayed.

In 1979, about six months after I left the Zen Center and re-established my life in the world, the nuclear issue came up for me again. I called a few people for advice, and they invited me to several meetings. I attended a Mobilization for Survival meeting where Randall Forsberg first presented the Freeze concept. I also met David Hoffman, who became a good friend — later we worked together on a big event called Survival Summer, 1980. I was off and running. I had finally found an arena where I could honestly say, "This is what I want to do!"

Before I got involved in the nuclear issue, if somebody had asked me, "What is your work really about?" I would have said, "friendship." During that time in my life, whenever I'd meet somebody I'd imagine another friend and think, "They'd really like each other!" But trying to connect them usually didn't work, because there was no context. After I got involved in the nuclear issue, every time I helped people to meet each other, the connection worked — because there was a context beyond us. So that's how I became a networker.

As I became an activist, I was struck by all my available financial resources. How could I do what I was doing and not put in my full share? At the Zen Center and in the anti-nuclear movement I had seen many people willing to commit their whole lives to issues they believed in. I realized that one of the things I could contribute, besides offering my organizing talents, was money. I was particularly drawn to funding individuals who were starting new projects, assisting them until their projects were better known and could be funded by others. Because I wanted to put myself on the line, I decided to go against the established ethos of never giving away financial principal.

I funded couple of people. It felt good, so I started travelling around the country, meeting activists and funding lots of projects. Over the next five years I gave away close to $750,000. I saw myself operating as a small personal McArthur Foundation, and imagined I would continue that way until I ran out of money. Over time, I developed a method of deciding what to support by trusting my inner voice. It was almost as though I didn't need to make a choice — my intuition guided me to what I had to do.

Since it had been so hard for me to find a work identity, my funding served a personal purpose as well — it established my identity as a networker and philanthropist. I was a catalyst, supporting other people to make key things happen. I had the good fortune to meet a lot of people that way, doing very exciting and important work. With almost everyone that I funded, I had a prior friendship. As I gave them money I knew it would change our relationship, but I trusted that it wouldn't harm it. This proved to be true — in fact, my funding was consistently a real joy.

In addition to all the grants, over the years I invested close to $500,000 in friends' creative and socially responsible business ventures. One friend, whom I had known for years, had developed an unusual model of how the body works and how cancer develops. I invested close to $120,000 in her business venture. Another friend was developing geothermal energy in Nevada. Another had come upon a new way of mapping the solar system. Another was researching pollution-control technology for processing toxic and chemical waste.

I haven't made money from any of these ventures, but some are still in business and may yet pay me back. If I did this kind of alternative investment over again, I would do more research and I'd pay someone to check out the investments for me. I also wouldn't do it alone, but would get co-investors. I was well-qualified to assess people in the public-interest arena, but not in business. Besides, part of my motivation in business was to prove to my father that I could make money as he did!

During that five-year period, I used my money to support people who did good work. The impact I was having was visible — people working on the nuclear issue said, "Hey, what you did for me really made a difference." The late '70s and early '80s turned out to be a significant time for raising consciousness and putting pressure on government leaders. I am glad to have been a part of it.

Part of what enabled me to give a lot of money away was living for years with minimal needs. My room at the Zen Center cost me $30 a month, my food was basic, my clothes were just enough to wear, and that was about it. I took any kind of job that came along; I never felt poor or deprived living that way. So I knew that if I ever gave away all my money I could live again in voluntary simplicity.

My philanthropy ended when I started a family, at age 40. I had been prepared to live the life of a Buddhist monk, but then along came someone I loved, with her daughter, and all of that changed. I let go of my fantasy of giving it all away. I got support from my friends and pressure from my family to stop giving the money away. My wife and I had another child.

I found other work I love to replace the philanthropy, and I fund myself to do it. I believe that we are our own best grantees — if we do work that we believe in and like doing. I wish we lived in a culture in which many more people could define what they want to do without worrying about earning a living. I would have to think very hard now before taking away my financial safety net and this freedom it gives me. Yet there's an old, wonderful dance between freedom and security — at times I feel as if I sold out by letting others influence me to stop before I gave all my wealth away. I alternate between having strong doubts and feeling fine about it, depending on my mood. It's a creative struggle.

Still, looking back on the philanthropy phase of my life, I feel wonderfully satisfied. I felt free to use money for what I believed in and what gave me joy. Once I started using money in the world in ways that matched my values, it was absolutely marvelous. It's hard to explain that. When I get together with other people of wealth, we tend to talk more about the difficulties, not about the fun. We don't have a lot of models of people who have given money away and just adored it. I like to be that model.

I would advise wealthy people to give to the point where they become anxious. In a state of discomfort there's a kind of questioning that goes on that's beyond the intellectual level, and that's where growth occurs. Give as if you're going to give it all away—and then seek guidance about when to stop. Ask yourself "Why am I on the planet; what's my role here? What's my best path of service?" When we ask ourselves these key questions, they offer a context in which to ask other questions: "Does this money serve, or does it get in the way?" That doesn't mean necessarily I give it all away—but it might. Ask yourself, "Does having money impede my growth, or serve my growth?"

Besides giving money away, work at the cause you believe in. Because if you're just a philanthropist, you miss something — you're separate from what you're giving to. I felt passionate about the antinuclear issue and about my deep friendships with the people I funded. It was a calling—in which I felt almost no choice; an outer pull and an inner drive meeting each other, a sense of order and rightness to my actions. I found situations in which I could give my money, my time, and my creativity simultaneously.

This was my way—I don't expect it to be the same for everybody. However, I do want to offer encouragement: take the risks that want to be taken! Be willing to make mistakes. Follow what your heart, your intuition and your whole being tells you. Be joyous with money! Have fun!

BETSY DUREN

Betsy is 30, and at the time of this interview worked for INFACT, a peace group organizing a boycott of General Electric because of its extensive defense contracts.

My father is a mathematics professor, and my mother is a trained librarian who works at home. They were very attentive to my brother and me. My mother would drive me every evening to the indoor track so I could run during my training. They were willing to make us the priorities of their lives.

My parents felt strongly that people should think for themselves. When I was in elementary school, if I went along with other kids on a prank my parents would be upset, not so much by the prank, but because I wasn't choosing my own course of action. I remember that the kids in our math class schemed to stand up all together at exactly the same moment, as soon as our teacher's back was turned, and then sit down again before she turned back around. For the life of her, she couldn't figure out what the giggles were about. I felt chagrined, and took my parents' lesson to heart. Once when I was a high school senior, all the students just walked out of a class, except me and one other person. I felt a little bit embarrassed because the teacher was probably wondering why I had hung around, but I felt it was the right decision.

In college at Bryn Mawr, I got involved in the feminist and lesbian communities on campus and worked for one of the school newspapers. Then, when I was 23, I inherited about $300,000 from my grandmother. While my family was upper-middle-class, we were not really rich, and we had seldom talked about the wealth in our extended family. When I inherited from my grandmother, my father worried I might have trouble handling it well and motivating myself.

After college I moved to Boston. A few days after I arrived I went to a concert of songwriter Betsy Rose. She sang about the threat of nuclear war, and about a young student who was just coming into the realization that maybe she could do something to make a difference in the world. I immediately identified and was very moved by the song.

I was staying at a cooperative house where a friend lived. The people in the house were very political, and I learned a lot from them about militarism and nuclear issues, sexual liberation, and civil disobedience. It felt safe to learn about the Boston radical community from them, because I trusted that my friend wouldn't live with weirdos, but with genuinely ethical people.

Over the next year or so I worked first at the Unitarian Universalist Association, and then as an editor for a journal of sexual politics — but I kept feeling there was something more useful I could be doing. Then, at another concert in May 1985, Betsy Rose announced that the "Pledge of Resistance" had been called. It was a pledge to take action whenever the U.S. government escalated its intervention in Central America. I signed the Pledge statement and later, I went through a five-hour training session in civil disobedience. I joined an affinity group, and, at the first call to action, I got arrested. It just felt right.

Ever since I first came to Boston, I felt it was likely that the world was going to blow up and that I was going to die along with everybody else. When I heard the Pledge had been called, it felt like I was being challenged to be brave and face my fears. It came very naturally; I felt ready for it. I felt that the Central America issue was an example of the U.S. trying to dominate another country economically in order to keep the standard of living in this country high, that U.S. intervention was helping cause war and human suffering all over the world. Opposing U.S. policy in Central America felt relevant and responsible. I wish I could say I am a brave person, but all I've done is what I felt I had to do at the moment.

I think that one of the most basic problems in our society is how much money is thrown into the military — more than half our income taxes go to support it. That's why I decided I would not voluntarily give the IRS anything, and in fact, I'd make it difficult for them to take it. At tax time, instead of sending a check to the IRS I sent a check for the same amount to the American Friends Service Committee, an organization that I believed would use it in the public interest. Eventually, the IRS started garnishing my wages, but then I found out from a war tax counselor that $75 per week is tax-exempt, so I asked my employer to cut back my pay to that amount. This stopped the IRS from collecting any money from me. Later I started free-lance computer work, and since I had no employer to take taxes out of my pay, it was easier to keep the money from the IRS.

My hope was that people who risked standing up to the IRS would help wake others up to how morally wrong it is for our tax dollars to build the military. I didn't want to give money to build weapons that can kill millions of people, and I can't pretend that my tax money is doing otherwise. The way I see it, people lack basic needs primarily because we are building military might to maintain U.S. economic domination over most of the world. The only way we're going to have lasting peace is by redistributing wealth. Poverty, war and suffering are caused by people who have more than their share of the pie trying to hold onto it.

*   *   *   *   *

Around the same time as starting tax resistance, I read *Robin Hood Was Right*, and felt galvanized into thinking about what I should do with my inheritance. I decided to get a job and support myself so I could give the money away. I went to a conference sponsored by Haymarket People's Fund for people with inherited wealth.

Although most people at the conference weren't thinking about giving away their wealth, the conference still made me feel I could give my money away. It helped a lot to know that other people didn't think I was crazy — even independent-minded people like me need a little backing!

The hardest part was telling my parents. My father was hurt that I was giving away the privilege he had given me. He compared it to immolating myself. My mother too, feared I'd regret this decision.

I told my father that I appreciated how he saved so I would have money. I was grateful for the privileges of a secure childhood and a good education — gifts I would keep all my life. I explained why I had to give away my money. I spoke about how accumulations of wealth result directly in human suffering, and about bearing public witness to these injustices. I talked with my father about wanting to help more people to realize that the U.S. war machine is wrong. That made sense to him, and my mother also shared my feeling that it's wrong for the U.S. to be dominating other countries. I tried to help her to understand that my giving away money was a way to counter the U.S. tendency to make the rest of the world live in poverty.

After the discussion with my parents, I added up all my financial assets. Stock, mutual funds, loans, and cash in the bank, added up to a little over $300,000. First I got totally out of the stock market, including mutual funds. I put all my money in several revolving community loan funds. The funds were very glad because I asked for no interest. This meant the funds could lend the money out to very low-income people who couldn't afford to pay back the money at high interest rates. Community-based revolving loan funds provide affordable loans and technical assistance to low-income people so they can buy homes. Investing in them felt like investing in an alternative economy. Like most upper-middle-class people, I was brought up to believe that if you have extra money, you should invest it to make more money. But once I decided the purpose of my money was to help the human community and help make peace, I no longer needed to invest to get the biggest profit, or even to make interest.

I even sold my stock in so-called "socially responsible" investments, like the Calvert Growth Mutual Fund. I know "socially responsible" investments have done some good — divestment, for instance, *has* made a difference in the South African situation — but frankly, I'm scornful of most "socially responsible" investments. For all their fanfare, they are merely the lesser of two evils. I decided I didn't want my money in any companies, traditional or "socially responsible," which profit wealthy stockholders at the expense of workers and consumers.

My plan was simple: as the community fund loans came due I'd give the money away. I decided to give away my principal over a five-year period. That seemed a reasonable time to learn how to give the money well, and to make sure I was ready to give up being wealthy. But as I proceeded with my plan, my confidence and conviction increased and I gave it away in four years instead. I couldn't do it quicker because I had placed large amounts in fixed-term community loans. I expected the last installment would be the scariest to give away. I had planned to keep a cushion of about $20,000, but as soon as the last loans came due in mid-1989 I gave away all but $7,000. It wasn't even scary — I had no hesitation, even though I was leaving my job and moving across the country. I kept the $7,000 to move, find a place to live, buy a computer and start my own business.

When I turn 35, I will get around $70,000 more from another trust, so I know this has allowed me to be more daring than I might otherwise have been. I'll have a few years to assess the results of my giving and how I feel about it before I decide what to do with this last chunk of money. I expect that I'll give it away as well.

I've always had a sense of what is enough. When I was ten years old I remember cleaning my room and getting rid of all the unnecessary things and extravagances and telling my parents, "Put these somewhere else in the house if you want them." They were surprised! Not only did I get rid of old clothes that didn't fit, I got rid of the framed pictures on my wall that my parents had chosen for me. I got rid of the rug. Later, I decided my dolls were a luxury and got rid of them too. I had this gut feeling that I wanted simplicity.

I was earning $600-800 per month at INFACT. I kept track of my expenditures and found that I consistently spent less than I earned. Even in the future I can't imagine I'll need more than $8,000 a year (in 1989 dollars) for day-to-day expenses. What would I need to spend more on? I've never wanted to acquire any of those things lots of people seem to want. For fun I read books and I hike in the mountains. I don't feel deprived; I like not having a lot of things. I feel unencumbered and free knowing if I want to move I can simply throw everything into a couple of boxes and do it. I own a computer, I have to admit, which gives me a tool to work with and a toy to play with.

I don't want such a low income that I would move into a total grow-your-own-vegetables situation. That would scare me. I'm currently earning about $700 per month so that I retain some independence. I am somewhat concerned about having money for retirement, but not too concerned just yet. I first want to do what I can to keep the world from blowing up, so I even have the chance to retire!

If I should suffer financial insecurity, I would not feel comfortable asking my family for money. I don't want to be a burden or seem irresponsible by asking for money after I had so much and gave it away. Asking for financial help scares me. No matter how close the people I ask are, I imagine my freedom would somehow be restricted. I guess my independence means more to me than just about anything. Yet I believe we need to give enough so that we're willing to risk falling back on other people.

For the first few years after inheriting wealth, I was *very* uncomfortable about having other people know I had money. I was afraid my fellow social-change activists would think I was different because I was rich and hypocritical for having all this money. I found myself sneaking out of work to pay phones and telling groups I'd funded not to call me at work. I felt that money was something I had to hide, and I think my bad feelings about myself affected other people.

Eventually, I stopped being secretive about having money. It is still sometimes scary wondering if somebody knows. But I've made a point of not keeping it secret, or lying about it. Now that I'm living my values more fully, I feel more legitimate in the movement — for being who I am. I think that comes across to other people too. I feel more self-respect for being honest.

I want to spread the idea of giving more principal. One day I went out to lunch with a man I've known all my life, a friend of my family. I didn't know he had inherited money until the middle of our conversation. We talked about it, and I tried to tell him what I had done without making it sound like I thought he was a jerk for not giving his money away. I just tried to tell him how good I felt about what I was doing. I think if people hear me talk about what I did, even if it comes across as overboard, it may encourage them to do something that seems less extreme to them but still significant.

Giving away my money has been good for me. I feel more confident and in control of my life; more genuine, too, now that I've let go of the money that others need so much more than I do. I'm pleased with the peace and justice work I funded. I'm more sensitive to people in need, now that I'm not insulated by having my money. And it feels good to be living what I believe, spending nearly all my time and money working to change the world in the best way I know how. If I somehow got the money back, I'd give it away again.

ROBBIE GAMBLE AND MARTHA MILLER

Robbie, an heir to the Proctor and Gamble fortune, and his wife Martha, gave away all the inherited wealth they controlled and founded a Catholic Worker house in Ontario, Canada. Since the interview, Robbie and one of his brothers returned from El Salvador, where they were investigating the oppressive conditions of coffee production for a shareholder resolution about the coffee at a Proctor and Gamble stockholder meeting.

Robbie: I grew up in Boston the oldest of three brothers. My mother was a homemaker, my father a cardiologist at Children's Hospital. I always thought we were a regular upper middle-class professional family, living off of my father's salary. Then when I turned 18, my parents took me out to dinner and said, "You are heir to part of the Proctor and Gamble fortune and you are a millionaire. You don't have to lift a finger for the rest of your life. Of course, we hope you do make something of yourself; we hope that the money will open up opportunities for you." I was totally floored.

Over dinner, I learned that Proctor and Gamble was started around 1820, and that my great-grandfather was the last Gamble to have a direct role in the company. Each of his three children inherited a million dollars. Of course, a million dollars was worth a lot more in those days. My grandfather got involved in the stock market and set up trusts to keep as much as possible from being taxed and to direct it to future generations. So, the money had a life of its own long before we came into the picture. Each of his 17 grandchildren would come into almost $3 million when they turned 18. That included me.

I grew up assuming that my parents would pay for my college and then I would be on my own. During high school I wanted to be an instrument maker and musical performer, and I had planned to study music at Harvard. After I found out about the money, self-sufficiency suddenly wasn't important any more.

I was 18 when I got full control over one of the trusts. I was not at all prepared. When the trust officer would say, "Would you like to do this or would you like to do that?" I would look at him and say, "What do you think?" He'd say, "I think you should do this." and I'd say "Sounds great to me!" Having the control didn't mean much.

My parents had made it clear I should talk about the inheritance only with them or with the trust officers — the last people in the world I wanted to confide in. I was a millionaire and supposed to feel thrilled about it, but I was not. It was a lonely time.

I was determined to make it easier for my younger brother, Jamie, and when he turned 18, I insisted that we break the news to him together. My father refused. This was how the information had been passed down to him, and he felt he had to uphold a tradition. I wouldn't give up. Eventually, we did it as a family with all five of us, including my youngest brother, Brad. My father made the presentation, but we were all there to take in Jamie's reaction and to support him. It worked out well.

*　　　*　　　*　　　*　　　*

In 1980 I had to make the vital moral decision of whether to register for the draft. I'd grown up during the Vietnam War, and I had seen on the news every night bloody pictures of a war that had gone nowhere. I knew deep down that I didn't want to take part in this draft, but the penalties for not registering were pretty stiff: a $10,000 fine and (more worrisome to me!) five years in prison.

I got involved with an anti-draft group in the Boston area. I started learning about the bigger issues, such as how the military consumes so much of our national resources that people are impoverished. The uneasy feelings I'd had about being wealthy started to crystallize. I realized that the wealth available to me to consume or keep within my family was denied to other people.

At this time, my faith started to emerge. While my family had regularly attended Episcopal Church and we had sung in the church choir, God and religion hadn't been important to me. But when suddenly faced with this dilemma, I realized that I needed to appeal to a higher power than myself. I took some courses on religious ethics and on moral and social inquiry. I was inspired by reading about the Catholic activist Dorothy Day. At Harvard I also met and was influenced by Robert Ellsberg, former editor of the Catholic Worker newspaper.

At a War Resisters' League conference on the draft, I met Jack Cook, who had been with the Catholic Worker in the early '60s and had been imprisoned for three years for advocating draft resistance. I was excited by him and others who had been activists over the long haul, and who had survived the kinds of things I feared. They had the larger moral picture I had been seeking.

I recalled that the summer I was 16, I had heard a speaker from a shelter for the homeless. As she was speaking, I felt suddenly that it was important for me to do similar work. I felt overwhelmed by the intensity of the feeling and went outside afterwards waiting for it to pass. At the time I was very seriously involved with music, and while this work with the homeless seemed very noble, I thought it wasn't for me. But by my final semester at Harvard, music had faded as a focus for my life, while faith and social issues had become increasingly important. So after I finished school I went on to the Catholic Worker in New York to volunteer.

I worked hard in the soup kitchen, and found work with homeless people fulfilling. My life felt much more integrated than it had for a long time. I discovered that living simply wasn't the hardship that I thought it might be. In fact, I found it very freeing in some ways. Not having to worry about lots of possessions enabled me to focus on more important things.

*　　　　*　　　　*　　　　*　　　　*

Martha: I was born in Northern Ontario, Canada. Our family wasn't poor — in terms of money we were average. We were a tight-knit family, Roman Catholic, with confession every Saturday and Mass every Sunday. I looked to religion to try to answer all my questions.

When I was 13, our family lived for three months in Pakistan. I was very shocked by the poverty there. We lived in Pakistan as rich people, in a separate community with other North Americans, with separate schools, and servants to work for us. It shocked me how much we removed ourselves from the local people and looked down on them.

One day I met a family who lived in a little three-sided house by the river. They had a baby who was sick, so I went home and stole three oranges to feed the baby. A couple of weeks later when I went to visit, the baby had died. I was stunned and confused. I didn't understand why the food hadn't saved the baby. I began to see that mere charity wasn't enough.

Over the years I became interested in working with poor people. A friend of mine gave me Catholic Worker newspapers to read. I was very taken — it seemed the purest form of the Gospel that I had ever seen before. So I decided to find out more about it.

I first met Robbie at the Worker house in New York. I had come to the soup kitchen to get something and in bounces this young, all-American boy, so eager and confident. We got to know each other and found we liked each other. We began a relationship.

In the fall of 1984 I left the Worker to go back to nursing school in Canada. Robbie got wise and chased me up to Canada a couple of months later. He stayed and we got more seriously involved. One day after supper he said, "There's something you should know about me." He looked so serious, I thought, "Gosh, maybe he is dying; why is he telling me this now?" He said, "I'm a millionaire." I was relieved that it wasn't anything terminal. Although, on second thought, it could be.

When I was first at the Worker I was dismayed with all the poverty I saw. I felt a righteous anger toward rich people. Then I married one!

Robbie's money first became real to me when we went to his money man's office. I was challenged trying to make sense of the financial concepts. For instance, I had no idea how he could be a millionaire — where was all the money? Robbie talked about it being such a struggle, but I couldn't understand that, either. If it was such a struggle, why couldn't he just give it away? But both his father and the finance man told him that he didn't have the legal power to give it away, and we both accepted that.

*　　　　*　　　　*　　　　*　　　　*

Robbie: As I became increasingly aware of the need in the world, I became certain that I wanted to give my money away. Living at the Catholic Worker, I realized that one can live well while living very simply. The richness of life came not from individual wealth, but from the support and love of a community of people living and working together in faith.

So I started doing more charitable giving. I was leading a double life, living where voluntary poverty was espoused and nobody was drawing a salary, and yet every so often I would go to Boston to sign trust documents and give away another $50,000.

Martha: It took me a long time before I could feel it wasn't just Robbie's money. One day I told Robbie I planned to send $40 from my next pay check to some friends of ours who had started a house of hospitality. Robbie said, "Well, you can send them $1,000, you know." I realized with a shock, that I could personally give large gifts to people. From that point on, when either of us heard of different projects, we would talk about them together and decide together about gifts. I still felt awkward. I mean, it was nice to be able to give so much, but I didn't feel at home with it. It stunned me! I was in this new league — I felt weird!

Robbie: I had been paying $100,000 a year in income tax. In 1983, after the U.S. invasion of Grenada, I decided I could no longer pay war taxes; U.S. foreign policy was just too crazy. So the next time the trust company filled out my tax return, I sent a cover letter explaining in moral and religious terms that I couldn't pay it. I refused to pay taxes three years until an IRS agent came to the trust company office and said, "We'll take this, this and this..."

Martha: As Robbie and I talked about our future: our marriage, our children, and the community, it naturally fell into place that we had to divest all that we could. It was incongruous with our vision of our lives to stay rich. We knew we didn't need it and the poor did. What had felt like a burden shifted to being more of a positive challenge. We were able to face trustees, lawyers, Dad, and other people who looked at us like we were crazy, and very clearly say to them, "This is what we want to do."

Robbie: When I told my parents I intended to give the money away, my father told me that I didn't have the power to do that. But while it is true I have some trusts that I don't control, and I'll probably be dealing with some inherited wealth for the rest of our lives, I realized that my father was just trying to discourage me.

My mother understands why I want to divest. She too feels weighed down by living in a large house and having lots of possessions, and in some ways would like to simplify her own life. My dad believes that his lifestyle and assets are justified by working hard, doing charitable giving, and passing the wealth on to the next generation. I think that for my father, the money and the family are so connected it's hard to separate them. We always had Crest and Ivory Soap in the bathroom — never Colgate! Their emotions are still tied up in Proctor and Gamble, even though they're not directly involved in the company.

Since I've been with Martha, I've been able to relax and realize I'm a person apart from the money. The trust money has gone from being a skeleton in the closet to something we can share with friends. It's strengthened us to be open about it, and we've been able to welcome the support and advice of friends. Although I've worried about not being loved or accepted because I have wealth, I've been very surprised at how accepting people have been.

Last year after we made a string of contributions, we got a phone call from the trust company from a woman with a strong British accent. She said, "Mr. Gamble, do you realize that you have dipped into your principal?" I could almost see the red lights flashing on and off, "Principal! Principal!"

Martha: The implied message we got was: "You are no longer a charitable man, you are a foolish man!"

Robbie: They were alarmed; we were thrilled. Our giving principal was just a natural continuation of our giving. In Canada, we made a major gift of $500,000 to establish a research center for community economic development. When we came back to the States, we went to the trust company and the trust officer said we weren't millionaires anymore. It was a great psychological barrier to cross.

Martha: Oh yeah! It was weird! We went into the office to find out how much we had left. The trust officer reported, 'You have "blah blah blah left" — $800,000 or something, and I started to feel anxious...It would be parallel to walking down the street thinking you had a $5 bill, and you put your hand in and it's only a $1 bill. Even though we intended the figure to go down, what ran through my mind was, "Oh. That's not very much!" That's when I saw that money can really convolute your entire perspective. Then I thought, "I guess we really *are* going to give it all away, aren't we!"

Robbie: We've now given away all of the trust money that we had control over. We have given to both friends and projects we knew about, and to projects or groups that we were convinced would bring about long-term change, rather than to traditional charities.

Of course we have given some money to soup kitchens, but we wanted the thrust of our divestment to support long-term change. Charity is needed but...

Robbie:...charity is dependency...
Martha:...and is not the deepest thing.

Robbie: We've given to projects such as land trusts and worker-owned cooperatives. We funded this Canadian development center which will create housing and jobs, and help people to be self-sufficient.

As far as living without the money, we've come to appreciate that precariousness is an important part of living. My aunts and uncles, although they are wealthy people, have experienced great pain and loss in their lives from which their wealth couldn't cushion them. My background of wealth has tried to erase the uncertainties of life. I feel challenged to accept that reality is uncertain, and I can't always be in control. Prayer helps me be open to this.

Martha: Wealth can't bring people together in marriage, and it can't bring dead people back. In the end, relying on others instead of on money is wonderful.

SHARING POWER AND PRIVILEGE

We give our money away in an effort to solve some of the many problems we see in the world. But is the *way* in which we go about our giving reinforcing the very injustices we're trying to change? Listen to these words from one of the founding fathers of modern philanthropy, Andrew Carnegie:

> This, then, is the duty of the man of wealth: To... administer [his funds] in the manner which, in his judgment, [will] produce the most beneficial results for the community — the man of wealth thus becoming the mere trustee and agent for his poorer brethren, bringing to their service his superior wisdom, experience, and ability to administer, doing for them better than they would or could do for themselves. [1]

While few of us who have money and who care about the world share Carnegie's blatant paternalism, many of us feel a tremendous sense of responsibility, and we assume it's up to us alone to make wise funding decisions. Consciously or unconsciously, we have absorbed some of the traits passed down through generations of upper-class people: assuming the weight of the world is on our shoulders (over-responsibility); believing we think better than others (arrogance); not asking for advice because we need to seem perfect (pretense); not trusting other people (isolation).

But this isolated decision-making often feels wrong.

> I have all this power to make [funding] decisions. The whole situation is nuts! It's unjust that anyone has so much power, and it's overwhelming to me to have such responsibility.
>
> — "Elinor Goldfarb"

Most of us are unaware that isolation is a class pattern, and it doesn't occur to us that we could act differently. Thus, we make our funding decisions alone, pouring over appeals and proposals in private, perhaps conferring with our spouse or a trusted financial advisor. But like Carnegie, even if we're supporting important projects, when we make our funding decisions without consulting others we are reinforcing one of society's historical power imbalances, where rich people make the decisions for others, especially for poor people.

Many of us, for example, want to fund work supporting the rights of various groups of disenfranchised people (e.g., Black, Latino, Native American), but few of us have lived or worked in those communities, or have asked the leaders of those communities about their own visions for change. Do we really want to use the power that comes with our wealth to decide, without their consultation, what's best for them?

People who are disenfranchised in society certainly welcome our financial support, but it's equally valuable to them when we also share the privileges we have due to our wealth. The power to decide where money goes is one of those privileges. Giving away wealth provides a wonderfully concrete opportunity to experiment with sharing power and privilege, by involving others in our funding decisions. How have donors done this? Here are three different approaches:

The Advisory Model: learning from others. In this model donors seek advice about what to fund and how much, but retain control over the final decisions. Some donors might talk extensively one-to-one with a variety of respected people, while others organize a group to discuss funding options. While some donors solicit advice from people who share their world view, others seek advisors from a wide range of political perspectives and life experiences. After listening to a variety of opinions, the donors decide what to fund.

> ...four people get together with me to help me make the [funding] decisions...One is involved with someone with inherited wealth; another is a working class person involved in international politics; the third is an older woman who is also a funder — she's a real mentor for me; and the fourth is someone with considerable experience as a staff member of a foundation...The group has been a sounding board and a place to strategize and discuss particular projects...It was great to show them how much money I had, groups I had funded, everything. When you get right down to it, however, I still decide.
>
> — "Elinor Goldfarb"

A few foundations operate "donor-advised" funds which are based, to a fair degree, on this advisory model. Typically, these are set up so that donors describe their funding interests to foundation staff members, who then prepare packets of proposals in those areas, inform donors about projects of special interest, and occasionally organize informational meetings on certain critical and underfunded areas. (See The Funding Exchange, Tides, and Partnership for Democracy in the Resource List.)

Even though this model limits shared decision-making power, it still enables people of different backgrounds to share their knowledge with us as funders and to often exercise substantial influence. Donors consider projects they wouldn't have known about on their own, and their thinking is enriched by the experience and perspective of others.

The Collaborative Model: sharing decisions with others. In this model, donors get together with others and make joint decisions about where the funds will go. They relinquish total control over the money, but remain active participants in all decisions. Whether a collaborative funding group involves people from a variety of class backgrounds or just brings together family and friends, it still challenges donors to trust the thinking of others.

> ...Over several years (of funding with others), I came to admit to myself that being with the other people was more gratifying than having the control and doing it alone. It was a big surrender for me to share control. When I stopped resisting it, I could see that the collective wisdom of the people in the foundation was greater than my own.
>
> — Ram Dass

The Threshold Foundation is an example of a group that combines the advisory and the collaborative models. Each year, over 100 people pool their donations (with added contributions from others) and serve on funding committees of 10-30 people. The committees submit and review proposals, make personal visits to each organization requesting support, and decide by consensus what to fund. Committees also receive advice and funding proposals from a professional staff.

Many members of Threshold have learned so much from this collaborative process, they call the foundation a "philanthropy university." Because each member is responsible to evaluate projects carefully, donors develop deeper knowledge and commitment to social change through the experience. For most, participation represents a major commitment to trust others and compromise, after years of making independent decisions.

The Community Empowerment Model: giving others the decision. In this model, donors relinquish all decision-making, and the funding is done instead by a multi-class, multi-racial board of community activists. Unlike most donors, these activist boards have extensive first-hand knowledge of the communities seeking funding. The model provides people of many backgrounds the opportunity to gain skills, knowledge and influence as funders. Many donors are happy to know that, without personally spending time on philanthropy, their money is being skillfully used for social change.

> I am not on the funding board of the foundation I set up because I believe in community activists having the control. I feel like the political message is important, enough that even though I am an activist too I bow out of the

grant-making process. It has been the greatest thing in the world! It allows me to just be an activist — I don't have to spend a lot of time working on the fund.

— "Sam Murphy"

The member funds of The Funding Exchange exemplify this model; each has a funding board of community activists. This stands in contrast to traditional foundations, where funding decisions are typically made by well-to-do executives and academics, not representatives of the communities to be served. People who give to The Funding Exchange get satisfaction from helping to build alternative institutions which embody non- classist values, and The Funding Exchange is proud of building a true partnership for change among people of all classes.

*　　　*　　　*　　　*　　　*

Class privilege is the practice of protecting the economic, political, and social benefits of one class while systematically denying such benefits to other classes. Some of these protected benefits should clearly be enjoyed by all — control over home and work place, access to a good education, influence in the political process. But a number of these protected benefits, while commonly accepted in our society perhaps should not be granted to anyone — for instance, the right to unlimited accumulation of wealth, and the right to own other people's homes or to control their working conditions. These privileges place a tiny minority's "right" to make money over the majority's right to a decent life. Eliminating classism means working to abolish these unjust privileges, while finding ways to secure the "essential privileges" for all.

At first glance, sharing decision-making about funding may seem unimportant. But the models above represent real ways to counter classism and decades of isolated and patronizing philanthropy. They are important experiments in sharing some of the power the class system confers to the wealthy few.

In addition to sharing funding decisions, those of us from upper-class backgrounds have other privileges we can share — education, self-confidence, skills, contacts with people of resources and influence. We can share these with organizations working to

build people's power. If our graduate-school education has made us capable essay writers, we can help write grant proposals for community groups. If our family has connections in Congress, we can use our name to give groups an "in." We can be most helpful not by taking over leadership, as many well-meaning people unconsciously do, but by learning to work behind the scenes, encouraging and supporting the leadership of others. Letting go of the need to be the one in control allows us to discover the beauty and power of being part of a diverse social change community in which all members are valued for their special contributions, and in which the whole is much greater than any individual part.

1. Carnegie, Andrew. *The Gospel of Wealth and Other Timely Essays*. Cambridge, MA: Harvard University Press, 1962, p.25. Although in this quote we highlight Carnegie's paternalism, we do recognize Carnegie's enormous contribution to philanthropy and to the communities he served, particularly through his creation of public libraries.

SPIRITUAL ECONOMICS

I can not picture to myself a time when no man shall be richer than another. But I do picture to myself a time when the rich will spurn to enrich themselves at the expense of the poor.

— Mahatma Gandhi [1]

At the heart of our giving is a desire to express love to others. Can we create economic relationships that model this spirit instead of the desire for personal gain that underlies our system of capitalist market economics?

Spirituality provides a context of values that guides our relationships with the other beings on this planet. Throughout history, spiritual traditions have taught that we should care for all others as ourselves. Economics is a set of societal rules about how we exchange resources. In recent history, one set of rules — capitalist market economics — has become dominant in this society. [2] But capitalist market economics does not provide consistent mechanisms for us to express our caring and support for one another — in fact it usually does the opposite. How do we deal with the dissonance this creates?

One response is to define and create a new economics — a spiritual economics, if you will. What would this spiritual economics be? It would be a set of societal rules about how we exchange resources which is congruent with diverse spiritual values. A spiritual economics would grapple with questions like these: How can we bridge the separation between self and other, giver and receiver? How can we balance our needs as individuals with our needs as part of a global community? How, acknowledging the political and technological complexities of our times, can we design new economic relationships based on what we can give to each other rather than on what we can get?

Many of us are struggling to bring our spiritual values and our economic relationships into greater harmony. Since we're doing this in the context of a capitalist market economy, we often feel out of kilter with the culture, like odd balls, alone and without guidance. Some of us seek guidance from religious teachings, which certainly have a lot to say about the dangers of caring more for material things than for our fellow human beings. Many modern religious leaders decry the materialism of our society:

> In our time the struggle of mercy is...not against rigid and inflexible morality, but against a different and more subtle hardening of heart, a general loss of trust and of love that is rooted in greed and belief in money. What irony that this faith in money, this trust in the laws of the market, this love of wealth and power, should have come to be identified with Christianity and freedom in so many minds, as if the freedom to make money were the freedom of the children of God, and as if...money had demonically usurped the role in modern society which the Holy Spirit is supposed to have in the Church.

> — Thomas Merton [3]

Most religious and spiritual traditions teach that individuals have a responsibility to give to those in need. The Jewish traditions of Ma'aser and Tzedakah, the Christian practice of tithing, and the Muslim practice of Zakat, all command the faithful to give 10% or more of their income to the needs of the wider community. And the Torah/Old Testament proposes a concept that goes far beyond simple charity: every 49th year we're to stop making money, to cancel all debts, to free any slaves, and to return all land to the original owner. This "Jubilee Year" is meant to be a time to celebrate the generosity of God and to demonstrate generosity towards others.

A number of religious teachers, including Jesus, Mohammed, Buddha, and Gandhi, explicitly urged (and themselves modelled) giving up wealth as an important element of spiritual dedication.

> Riches are not from an abundance of worldly goods, but from a contented mind. It is difficult for a man laden with riches to climb the steep path that leadeth to bliss.

> — Mohammed [4]

Again and again, spiritual traditions teach that our relationships to family, community, the earth, and God are more important than material wealth, and that wealth may actually divert us from genuine fulfillment. But few of us searching for a spiritual economics are prepared to give all our money away. Aren't there less drastic ways to bring our actions and values into greater harmony?

Some traditions suggest an attitude of "stewardship," in which we acknowledge that our surplus resources belong to the community. We are not the "owners" of those resources, but rather their trustees.

Complete renunciation of one's possessions is a thing which very few even among ordinary folk are capable of. All that can legitimately be expected of the wealthy class is that they should hold their riches and talents in trust and use them for the service of the society.

— Mahatma Gandhi [5]

He that cleaves to wealth had better cast it away than allow his heart to be poisoned by it; but he who does not cleave to wealth, and possessing riches, uses them rightly, will be a blessing unto his fellows. It is not wealth and power that enslave men, but the cleaving to wealth and power.

— Buddha [6]

Many of us find that this idea offers us guidance in our quest for a spiritual economics.

We have been put here with a particular set of resources. For some people it's great creativity, and for others . . . practical skills. For some . . . it's money. Whatever the resources are, we are enjoined to use them for the benefit of society.

— Joe & Teresina Havens

Whenever I get confused about my money and how to deal with it, I get a lot of clarity and perspective when I stop and think that it's not my money. Instead I view myself as a spiritual aspirant who has been entrusted with a large sum of money by God, and that my work is to learn how to utilize this money in a way that is both beneficial for my own spiritual development and of service to humanity.

— "Rob Stoner"

But even if we manage to act reasonably well as stewards for our resources, how do we deal with the wider society, which currently embodies a very short-sighted set of values? Native traditions urge people to consider the impact of their decisions on the seventh generation after their own. [7] This stands in stark contrast to the economic decisions made today by corporations pushing constantly to provide their share holders with a sizable profit for the next annual meeting. In the pressure of the capitalist market economy, leaders make decisions with grave consequences for our children and grandchildren. If human beings and the earth are true priorities, spiritual values and practices such as trusteeship need to be integrated into our society and economic structures. A spokeswoman of feminist spirituality describes a vision of such an integration:

The structures of society that create health are really pretty simple...In such structures everything is valued for what it is, in and of itself, not in its relationship to some external factor like profitability. That's a spiritual value...In groups and institutions that's just not an abstract idea; it means that when decisions are made each person's opinion and view and needs are taken into account and — as much as possible — are met.

— Starhawk [8]

Even though the society as a whole is far from integrating economics and spiritual values, many people are developing alternative institutions — community-controlled foundations, alternative businesses, community loan funds, barter networks, community land trusts, worker-owned and operated businesses, and mutual aid funds, to name a few — that embody some of the community-affirming economic principles. A number of social movements are promoting consciousness of these values in mainstream economics: The environmental movement is creating pressure for more government and corporate accountability towards our environment. Firms on Wall Street are beginning to respond to their investors' advocacy regarding investment in South Africa, nuclear power, and involvement of women and peoples of color in corporate positions of influence. Groups like the Social Ventures Network and the Organizational Transformation Network are bringing together business people who want to bring their business lives into alignment with their deepest caring for the world. These are a few of the signs of change, and each one of us seeking to put spiritual economics into practice adds momentum to the spreading of new, values-based economic structures.

*　　　*　　　*　　　*　　　*

If you are attracted to the idea of putting spiritual economics into practice, but aren't sure how to start, here are some suggestions:

Listen inside. Find time to listen to the spiritual voices that have meaning for you, whether they are voices within, historical figures you admire, spiritual teachers, or some other source of wisdom. Seek out examples of people who inspire you with their courage, vision and hope. Spend time alone, in prayer, in meditation, in communion with nature.

Allow suffering. Let yourself not know what to do. Although many of us lead our daily lives as if we don't care about the world's suffering, the truth is most of us care deeply. When we see the enormity of human suffering on TV and in newspapers and feel powerless in comparison, it can hurt so much that we despair and turn off. Why should we make those people real, when there's nothing we can do? So we close our hearts.

> The human race is our family, but we are often afraid to recognize that truth for fear we will be overwhelmed by the pain and suffering all around us. So we armor our hearts and deny our kind. The cost of such armoring is great indeed. To others, it denies them our caring and our resources; to ourselves, it denies us the sustenance of spirit that comes only when boundaries between self and other dissolve in love. People who do good because they can't stand the pain of suffering are not going to do much, because the suffering is bottomless. You must be able to embrace suffering in yourself and be joyful even in the presence of suffering and then do what you do.

— Ram Dass [9]

Most of us were taught to close our hearts to others many years ago, when we were children. Learning to open again and to "embrace suffering" may be a long process. Take the time to notice your reactions to humanity's pain. (There are many opportunities — reading the paper, riding the bus, listening to a friend's troubles, contemplating human history...) Notice how you either want to rush in and fix it, or you want to push it away. Notice how hard it is to just be with what is, allowing your heart to connect yet not needing to change a thing. The repeated practice of opening your heart is an important step in reclaiming your connection to the world. (Two useful resources in this process are *Despair and Empowerment in the Nuclear Age* by Joanna Macy, and *How can I Help?* by Ram Dass and Paul Gorman).

Get support to take concrete steps. Talk with people you know about what's on your mind and in your heart. Your aim is to find at least one person, a kindred spirit, who shares your search. That someone may be an old friend or you may need to look to new friends. Try meeting people through the social concerns committee at a local church or temple, through a service organization in your neighborhood, or by contacting one of the organizations listed in this book.

Once you've spent a while opening your heart, sitting with the pain of caring and not knowing what to do, ideas will come to you about how you might change your life. There's no shortage of actions to take; the books in the bibliography are full of ideas. What most of us need is not more good ideas, but help to sort out our ambivalences, to find what speaks to us, and to put our ideas into practice. Use your friend in the venture to help you do this. Take a small step and talk about how it feels. Take another small step. Be patient with yourself, and keep searching for ways that speak deeply to your heart, so that you can use your gifts (money, intelligence, compassion, skills) to contribute in ways that feel fulfilling to you.

Integrate your values with your life. Little steps build, and over time, more and more of your daily life reflects your deeper values: how you spend money, what you do for work, your relationships with family and friends, and what you do for fun. As spiritual economics becomes integrated into your life, you may find your support network changing: that initial island of support becomes a whole community of people who love and respect you, who help bring out the best in you, and who challenge you to keep taking risks that enrich your life and serve a common future. This, truly, is wealth.

> Pass the money through you in a way to heal the universe. Listen to what heals—have your life serve as your message. The way you live is the way to do it!
>
> — Ram Dass

1. Fisher, Lewis, ed., *The Essential Gandhi*. New York: Random House, 1962, p. 284.

2. For more on another economic structure: a "gift economy" see the first few chapters of Hyde, Lewis, *The Gift*. New York: Random House 1983.

3. From *Love and Living* quoted in Ministry of Money newsletter #50, 10/87.

4. Mead, Frank Spenser. *The Encyclopedia of Religious Quotations*. Old Tappan, NJ: Revell Co., 1966. From *The Sayings of Mohammed*, Wisdom of East Series.

5. Fisher, *op. cit.*, pp. 284–85.

6. Carus, Paul, ed., *Buddha: His Life and Teaching*. New York: Crescent Books (no date given).

7. Myers, Mike. "A Native American Philosophy and Perspective of Development." unpublished article. Lee, NV: The Seventh Generation Fund, October 1989.

8. Starhawk. "Being the Energy: Spirituality, Politics and Culture." in Plant, Judith and Christopher Plant, eds., *Turtle Talk: Voices for a Sustainable Future*. Philadelphia: New Society Publishers, 1990, pp. 33–34.

9. From the Seva Foundation *1987 Annual Report*.

OUR GIVING MAKES A DIFFERENCE

It means a great deal to those who are oppressed to know that they are not alone. And never let anyone tell you that what you are doing is insignificant.

— Bishop Desmond Tutu

In the face of vast social problems, it's easy for our giving to feel utterly insignificant, no matter how much money we have. Most of us are deluged by direct mail appeals, confronted by poor people begging for change, urged by canvassers at our door to sign their petition and donate a few dollars to their cause. Sometimes we give and other times we don't, but it rarely feels as if it makes much difference.

In order to undertake the challenging work of conscious giving, however, we need to believe our individual contributions *do* make a difference. How is it that those of us who have shared our stories here came to believe that our giving mattered? Many of us had experiences early in life that gave us both a personal taste of injustice and a glimpse of what people working together can accomplish. These experiences gave us important motivations — of outrage and of hope. As we searched for ways to create a more just society, we were confronted with a humbling but empowering paradox: while it takes the commitment of millions of people across all races and classes to transform society, unless each one of us does what we can individually, no collective effort exists. In creating social change, concrete results often take generations to achieve and consolidate. Just as every social movement is composed of individual people, each sweeping advance is the culmination of many small, barely noticeable changes. We came to understand and believe that individuals like us are essential to work the tiny changes that make up the vast whole.

For us, this meant coming to a decision to give away some or all of our principal. In some ways, it seemed a small act, compared to the sacrifices others we knew were making for the causes they believed in. But even this relatively safe choice was questioned by other activists and funders, who worried about what would happen if wealthy people committed to social change depleted their resources, leaving insufficient funds in the future.

Their challenges helped us to articulate what we were discovering through our choices: that strategic and substantial giving can actually increase the resources available for progressive change. Many of us have used our money to set up or strengthen progressive foundations. Those foundations reach thousands of new donors and provide a far more reliable funding base for social change than individuals ever can. By placing substantial assets in tax-exempt structures such as donor-advised funds or foundations, more money is available overall to fund projects because no taxes are taken on capital gains or income. Donors also get personal tax deductions for their gifts, and the funds or foundations are able to invest the money with greater flexibility, without the concern of income tax liability.

And committed giving may actually be just what others need to see to take heart and give more themselves.

> After ten years the fund will be exhausted; that's exactly the plan. Doesn't that hurt the ability of the fund to keep providing resources for social change? If our political message is clear enough and our political work is important enough to the community, somebody will donate money to revive the fund or be inspired to establish a similar fund.
>
> — "Sam Murphy"

Beyond these considerations, giving principal makes sense to us because we believe that money given now on critical social and environmental problems can help prevent drastic deterioration that will cost far more to solve in the future.

*   *   *   *   *

No matter how much you have to give, it makes sense to give strategically — to deepen and multiply the impact that your money can create. Here are some suggestions about how to accomplish this:

Learn to be a skillful giver. Stick with an area of funding for at least several years, and get to know the organizations doing good work in that area. Find out about their progress — including how they cope with problems of organization, finances or program. Evaluate your giving and think each year or two about how to improve it.

For example, one funder decided to focus on human rights. She discovered that the national group she had always funded already had ample resources, and that a city-wide group she learned about could make better use of her contributions. Over the years, as she became knowledgeable about the group's successes and struggles, she was able to make a few specific and timely grants that made a real difference in the organization's effectiveness.

Learn about the structures that are available for charitable giving. If you intend to donate a substantial amount of money over several years, setting up a donor-advised account within an established foundation can offer you several advantages. Here's how it works: You donate the whole amount up front to the foundation (and get a tax deduction for it), and the foundation's staff set up a fund in your name or in the name of your choice. Then, over the following months or years, you let them know the organizations to which you'd like to contribute from your fund. Although the foundation has the legal right not to accept your grant recommendations, unless there is some special problem your suggestion will ordinarily be accepted. The income your fund generates is tax-exempt (so there's actually more money to give away) and staff will often help you find and evaluate projects in your particular area of interest. This can be valuable, since foundations are aware of many effective projects that you might not know about. (The Funding Exchange and Tides Foundation both provide this service — see Resource List for contact information.)

In addition to donor-advised funds, there are many other structures available, including wills and charitable trusts. Part of being a skillful giver is knowing the pros and cons of these different structures and making a long-term plan for your giving. You can ask The Funding Exchange or a member fund near you to send you a free copy of *Creative Ways to Give*, their easy-to-read booklet describing many of these options. After considering the different approaches, you might consult a financial advisor and/or a lawyer if the plan you have in mind is complex.

Use your own giving (and contributions of time, skills and energy) to attract donations from others. When you decide to contribute to a project, send a letter and brochure about the project to friends who might be interested and offer them the chance to contribute, too. Or invite friends (including those without substantial money) to join you in pooling money, each contributing anonymously at an appropriate level and then together contributing the pooled sum to projects in an area of common concern. Or set up a donor-advised fund and invite others to participate.

> I set up a fund because my funding seemed like a long-term project and because I wanted to create a vehicle my siblings might contribute to. In fact, my brother just put money into it. He's a scholar and is sorry that he does not have time to go out and put his values directly into action in the world. Giving to this foundation was an opportunity for him to take action that he felt good about.
>
> — "Elinor Goldfarb"

Help establish progressive public foundations. Doing so not only attracts new donors, but may inspire others to start similar funds. As an individual, George Pillsbury helped to start The Funding Exchange, which in turn has helped donors and community activists set up similar community foundations. Other individuals played key start-up roles in The Women's Foundation Network and in several of the Black United Funds. These networks, which serve particular constituencies rather than just specific locales, have activated thousands of new donors. Many other constituencies are still underfunded, and many poor geographic areas lack progressive funds in their area; there is plenty of room for more foundations. And you don't need vast sums to do it. You can bring together a number of donors to pool the initial seed money and the foundation can fundraise for ongoing operation. Contact The Funding Exchange if you are interested in how to go about it.

Use your influence to bring together other potential givers, for education and peer support. After returning from a trip to the Middle East, one funder organized an evening where friends and allies learned about dynamic Middle East projects they could support. Another group of funders commissioned a research project to discover whether well-known sports, media and business personalities might become involved in social change funding. [1] Their study has stimulated several experiments for attracting new funders.

Others have organized support groups in which members help one another deal with their personal issues about money and become more effective in their giving. Group members can encourage each other to learn more about social change — for instance, setting up a 6-week study group on an issue of common interest.

Help with more than money. You can assist groups with their fundraising. For instance, you could offer to pay for a group to improve the appearance (and fundability) of their materials (e.g., graphics, laser printing), or enable a staff person to attend workshops on fundraising. If you have writing skills, you could volunteer to edit grant proposals drafted by others. If you have a spacious home, you could offer to host a fundraising party and invite some of your friends. You could purchase a small collection of books about fundraising and loan these as a resource to various groups. [2] These are only a few examples of the many ways you can improve the financial health of organizations you care about, whether or not you personally give much money to them.

*   *   *   *   *

It's true that, at times it seems very discouraging. When we look for improvement in huge social problems, it may be hard to identify any results from our giving, and all too often the big problems only seem to be getting worse. But in grassroots organizations, a little money at the right time can make an enormous difference. Examples of this are numerous: the $200 for bail that freed a Native American activist who had been unfairly imprisoned...the $1000 gift that enabled a visiting organizer from the Polish Solidarity movement to purchase several old copy machines to take back home — who knows what role these machines played in the success of that movement?...the three-month loan of $2,000 that let a housing organization avoid the layoff of their only staff member during a severe cash flow crunch...the modest "seed grant" that helped a new environmental group get started and grow into a strong organization with national clout that now does funding of its own. No matter how large or small the amount, when you contribute to grassroots groups, your giving makes a difference. And it is the efforts of thousands of these groups that create social movements. Ultimately, over time, social movements share history.[3] If you think strategically about your giving, you are bound to have an impact — probably more than you will ever know.

> No ray of sunshine is ever lost
> but the green it awakens into existence
> needs time to sprout
> and it is not always granted
> for the sower to see the harvest.
> All work that is worth anything
> is done in faith. [4]

1. Guyer, Cynthia. "Developing New Sources of Progressive Philanthropy." New York: HKH Foundation, 1990.

2. A few resources to start off a lending library on social change fundraising: Klein, Kim. *Fundraising for Social Change*. Inverness, CA: Chardon Press, 1988. National Network of Grantmakers. *Grant Seekers Guide*. Mt. Kisco, NY: Moyer Bell Ltd., 1989 (write to them for the most recent edition: Colonial Hill/RFD 1, Mt. Kisco, NY 10549). Center for Third World Organizing, *Activist's Guide to Religious Funders*. Oakland, CA: Center for Third World Organizing, 1990 (write to them: CTWO, 3861 Martin Luther King Jr. Way, Oakland, CA 94609). Also, get a complete listing of members of The Foundation Center, a national network which provides library reference collections for free public use. Write to: The Foundation Center, 79 Fifth Ave., New York, NY 10003.

3. For more information about how social movements develop see: Lakey, George. *Powerful Peacemaking*. Philadelphia: New Society Publishers, 1987. Moyer, Bill. "The Political Strategist," San Francisco: Social Movement Empowerment Project, 1990. (available for $3 from SMEP, 721 Shrader St., San Francisco, CA 94117. Cooney, Robert and Helen Michalowski. *The Power of the People: Active Nonviolence in the United States*. Philadelphia: New Society Publishers, 1987.

4. Source unknown.

DOING A LOT WITH A LITTLE

I don't do any great thing; I do small things with great love.

— Mother Teresa [1]

"But I'm not wealthy! How can my puny check count for anything?"

Most people doubt that their contributions will make much difference, whether they are as rich as the Rockefellers, comfortably middle-class, or scrimping to make ends meet. Monetary wealth can be measured objectively, but how wealthy one feels is very subjective. Even a homeowner with a savings account may feel poor compared to others who have more. On the other hand, that same person in a poor country might be wealthier than most people there can imagine. More than how much money one has, how ample it feels influences what one does with it.

> If I had a million or even a hundred million dollars it still wouldn't change the world. So I'll just do what I can with what I have.

— "Richard Moulton"

For those who long to contribute towards a better world but don't know where to start, here are some practical approaches that work. Even meager resources can great impact, both to oneself and to the world. Addresses for all the resources are in the Appendices of the book. Experiment and have fun!

Choosing wisely where to shop and bank. Money has clout in this society, especially when it is directed in an organized way toward specific goals. The power of a large number of consumers is a force to be reckoned with — which is why where you spend (and don't spend) matters. Boycotts, even when they start small, can be effective: for example, many tuna companies have changed their fishing practices to assure the safety of dolphins, largely from the pressure of organized consumers refusing to buy their tuna. Find out about current boycotts from the quarterly journal "Building Economic Alternatives." Many shoppers are using the book Shopping For a Better World which lists hundreds of common products and describes the environmental, military and social practices of the companies that produce them. With the guide you can purchase goods from companies whose practices you support and avoid the others. Increasing numbers of mail-order companies market goods that promote social justice and environmental care — for instance, Pueblo to People and Co-op America.

Even with a modest bank account, where you bank makes a difference. For instance, banking by mail with the South Shore Bank in Chicago or the Community Capital Bank in Brooklyn, N.Y., even a small checking or savings account will help develop housing and businesses for low-income people. And you can earn interest comparable to money market funds by lending money to community loan funds such as the Institute for Community Economics Revolving Loan Fund in Springfield, MA. The National Association of Community Development Loan Funds can help you find a fund near you. These funds provide technical assistance and affordable loans to low-income groups.

Making satisfying contributions. Is your mailbox incessantly holding requests for money? Does it sometimes feel like groups spend your $25 contribution for postage and printing of never-ending appeals? Do you wonder what great groups might be out there that can't afford to fundraise by mail? Perhaps you'd like to find a more satisfying way of giving money to worthy causes.

As a first step, figure out your total of your contributions last year — through direct mail, religious affiliation, United Way payroll deductions, canvassers, Salvation Army buckets, and so on. Or guess about the total amount you would like to give this year.

Next, list some of the groups you have given to in the past, and think about why you give to those places. Some common reasons are: personal ties ("My uncle died of cancer so I always give to the United Cancer Drive."); connection to an issue ("I've been scared about nuclear war since I was a kid, so I give to The Nuclear Disarmament Group."); a desire to belong ("I feel more a part of my community since contributing to Clinton Center for the Arts."); critical timing in relation to desired changes in the world ("I think what occurs in Eastern Europe now will influence all of our futures, so I'm giving to the Eastern Europe Democracy Fund."); loyalty, habit, and peer pressure

("I've given to my college every year for twenty years. How could I stop?") and emotions, such as feeling guilty or inspired ("Their appeal letter was so moving I just had to write a check.") The point is not to judge any reason as good or bad, but just to notice the different needs your giving fills. Try to find other reasons than the ones listed here.

Now with a clearer sense of how much and why you want to give, you can plan better your giving. It may feel most satisfying to prioritize the groups that mean the most, and get off the mailing lists of the others. Say you gave $300 last year: $25 each to 8 groups and $10 each to ten groups. This year, you could still give ten $10 contributions to groups where you feel personal loyalty, combined with two $100 contributions to groups you've chosen more carefully. $100 doesn't mean much to a huge national group, but in your community there are probably many struggling, innovative organizations that would rejoice in your $100 contribution.

Also, instead of responding to requests that come knocking, take a proactive approach: tell friends about areas of interest and ask what groups they support; call funding agencies and get their suggestions about organizations. Since mail appeals are essentially advertisements (and so don't reveal much), gather more information about the groups to consider. Most groups would gladly send details about their operations, including specific goals for the coming year and copies of financial statements. After reading a few groups' materials, you can see which groups are well-organized and what more there is to know about them.

Sometimes giving feels impersonal — you write a check, and who knows what happens? Many people find it more satisfying to give where they can develop a personal relationship. Visiting or volunteering with local groups can make your giving feel increasingly meaningful. There are also ways to give which specifically develop relationships with activists or groups. Several are reminiscent of "Save the Children" in their personal approach, but are oriented towards providing critical support for those taking leadership for social change in the Third World. For example, as part of the Partner's Project, David, who makes about $12,000 per year, puts aside $30 each month to send to a woman in India. This money completely supports her full-time work organizing land and housing for low-income people. Another group, Ashoka, finds creative grassroots leaders in struggling countries and assists their work by providing them publicity and funding. Sponsoring an Ashoka Fellow can include developing a relationship with the person.

Another way to experience greater impact is to pool money with others. For example, if combatting prejudice and discrimination has always meant a lot to you, invite ten friends who share that concern to make an anonymous contribution to a common pot. Perhaps an individual donation might be $100 — now there's $1,500! Then the ten get together for an evening, discuss different groups doing anti-discrimination work, and jointly decide what to fund. Through this type of pooled giving, you can learn more about some good causes, take part in a substantial donation, and share an interesting evening with friends, all at the same time. In a town in California, one family organized ten families to pool $100 each, and those ten families each organized another ten...now they've become an ongoing group that gives $10,000 annually to community projects. An even easier way to pool money is to give to a community foundation. Just as mutual funds pool many people's investments and allow informed professionals to make the investment decisions, so community foundations pool many people's giving and allow informed community activists to make the funding decisions. By contributing this way your money can help fund hundreds of groups creating change. Some foundations give to a wide range of issues (for example, The Funding Exchange makes grants in many areas, including social justice, anti-racism, women's issues, and gay and lesbian rights) while other funds focus on one area (for instance, The Women's Foundation supports projects which empower women and girls).

Living your values. One way to do a lot with a little is to deliberately live a simpler lifestyle. Why live more simply? On the global level it's like taking your fair share at dinner: no one has a second helping until everyone has a first. For the U.S. to cut down to its fair share of global resources, the majority of its citizens will need to switch to a way of life that is satisfying with far less consumption of material goods. Modelling a simpler life helps show that this is desirable and possible.

On the personal level, living more simply can reduce expenses, giving you the flexibility to work at lower pay (lots of good work in the world is not well paid) or to contribute more money to people or groups. Many ways of living more simply (for example, riding a bike to work instead of driving) are also more environmentally sound. And many people who have chosen to live more simply have found it spiritually and emotionally more satisfying than their previous lifestyle.

It is possible to have ample material goods while still living more simply by sharing resources with others. A group of neighbors can share one lawn mower and one snow blower instead of every family having their own; several friends who live near each other can co-own a computer and work out a system or schedule for each person's use. By sharing possessions people often can have more than they could individually afford. In many parts of the country, clusters of people are organizing "co-housing communities" based on this premise. In a co-housing arrangement, 15-30 households get together to plan a mini-village. Together, they buy land, build and manage their own residential community. Each household has its own small but complete home, while enjoying use of the community resources: a large common house, usually equipped with an ample kitchen, dining hall, recreation room, child care area, guest and laundry facilities, and tool shop. Besides making more amenities affordable, sharing resources builds a real sense of community and mutual support.

Living more simply does not mean becoming an ascetic. It means discovering ways to nurture yourself through love, health, friendship, nature, service and creativity, instead of through buying more things.

Sharing your energy. Involvement in important issues can make far more difference than a check, no matter what its size. If your cry is "But I'm too busy!" you're not alone; that's why some social change groups have designed projects with the over-committed in mind. You can help release political prisoners in a minute a month, by letting the Rapid Response Network send protest telegrams in your name to government officials responsible for prisoner's release. (The minute is the time it takes to pay the bill, which can be billed to a credit card.) With just $20 a year and 20 minutes a month, you can have clout in Congress: each month the organization 20/20 Vision will send you a postcard with a suggested action (usually a letter or phone call) to influence peace or environmental legislation. Because hundreds of others are responding together, you know the collective voice will be heard. Browse the book *How to Make the World a Better Place* for other valuable action ideas.

Volunteering a few hours a month can be personally enriching, and make you feel part of movements for change. If you're confused about where to start, talk to a friend whose work you admire and ask if you can help; join The Giraffe Project, which sends newsletters filled with inspiring stories of people who "stick their necks out" for the common good; think of something enjoyable — writing? baseball? cooking? talking? — and volunteer in those areas. Because economic injustice is held in place by people being isolated and fearful of each other, try something that creates personal contact across class lines.

Building communities of support. Taking steps to align your life and your values is surprisingly hard. Even switching to a different brand of light bulb can be a major effort! Life has a momentum of its own, filled with habits and daily crises that make it hard to start anything new.

Unless you are an unusually motivated and independent sort, the most important way to support your goals is to join with others with similar values. Talk about the ideas here. Share questions and issues. Choose a tiny goal, a small step you can do this week or the next, and talk later about the success or difficulty achieving it. Set another tiny goal. It doesn't matter whether you set up something as casual as a monthly talk with a friend over coffee, or as formal as a weekly activist support group. To live with growing integrity and power, we need each other's help.

Mending a society wounded by generations of inequality and injustice does not happen overnight. However, change is not linear: it may seem as if nothing is changing for a long time, and then suddenly, a great change just seems to happen. When this occurs, it is because the small actions of many people over time have eroded the injustices which seemed unchangeable.

> It's not just what you're born with,
> But what you choose to bear
> It's not how large your share is,
> But how much you can share
> It's not the fights you dream of,
> But those you really fought
> It's not just what you're given,
> But what you do with what you've got.
>
> — Si Kahn [2]

1. As recounted by Frank Butler who met with her at the Mother House in Calcutta on a Ministry of Money trip.

2. On his "Unfinished Portraits" recording. Joe Hill Music.

TRACY GARY

Tracy co-founded The Women's Foundation, where she has worked for over ten years running a program helping women learn to manage inherited wealth. Tracy has been promoting the development of similar programs nation-wide.

My mother was related to the Pillsburys. She divorced my father when I was $4\frac{1}{2}$ and shortly thereafter married Theodore Sauvinet Gary, whose grandfather had invented the dial telephone and whose family was extremely wealthy. In the meantime, my mother had made considerable money in the stock market and had inherited more from her own family.

The first time I realized my family had more money than other people was the first day of school in first grade when the teacher said, "Where do you live?" It was immediately clear to me that I was different. Although many families in our private school had second homes out on Long Island, our family had four or five houses, which seemed more than other people. They employed up to 45 people to run these houses — quite a large number of people for me, as a child, to relate to.

This feeling that I was different increased as I got older. More often than not I was taken places by the chauffeur instead of by my mother or father. Domestic workers and nannies came to family days at school. At times I loved the excitement of a jet set life, but when my parents came to visit me at boarding school in a helicopter or picked me up at graduation in a yellow Rolls Royce, I felt very conspicuous and alienated from the other kids. A Black woman named Nellie took primary care of me from the time I was born. Since my parents were gone easily half to three quarters of the year, it was very important to me that Nellie was as constant as she was. I would not have become a caring and feeling person without her. When I was 11, I asked my stepfather how much Nellie was getting paid. She was working 60 hours a week, and had almost no time off. It turned out that she was making $75 a week plus room and board. I was shocked because I loved her and it seemed so unfair. Her family had been with my mother's family for generations. The incongruity between what Nellie had and what my parents had just snapped something in me.

When my parents traveled I was left with one or two domestic workers in a house with 30 rooms. I was tremendously arrogant, a little princess. When my parents were present, half of the time they were recovering from having been gone. If you have five houses and you're dealing with two to 25 staff people at each of those houses, and dealing with your mail, with your jet lag, and with your kids, there is a certain amount of chaos. It was a great environment to learn how to socialize with people, because I was having buffet dinners with 20 people most of the time. I've had meals alone with my parents probably ten times in my entire life.

I used to love going to my friend Penny's house, because her family sat down to dinner together—with brothers, sisters and parents. When I came over, they played games at the table, and they'd ask questions like "What happened today?" and "How are you feeling?" to get to know me. It was such a different experience from my family.

From the time I was seven, we went every summer to an island in Wisconsin. In the winter, the population was about 200, mostly Native American, but in the summer there were another thousand people. My great-grandfather had been the first white man on this island, so my family played a special role.

We employed a lot of the people who lived on the island all year long. Every summer my parents renovated an old building for community use: an old school was turned into a health center; another building became a library; another a museum for the little island. I saw how my parents worked with the community, and I understood that giving to others was very much expected of me. I worked in the library every summer covering books, and taught kids how to read. I got paid for some work, but it was clearly important to my parents that I also volunteered.

As time went on I had some occasional difficulties with my stepfather. The messages I got from him were contradictory: "It's very important that you work with everybody," but "Maintain your superiority." The neighborhoods we lived in were very exclusive. My stepfather was head of a country club which did not accept Jews and Blacks as members. I was aware of a distinct difference in my parents' attitudes towards us and towards people different from us, including Jews and people of color. That created a conflict for me, because some of those "different" people were the very people they entrusted to take care of me.

In response to his prejudice, I was drawn to kids who were different from me. I began to play in the summers with kids who were Native Americans and "Islanders." The telephone operator's daughter was my best friend. Both her parents were alcoholic, but brilliant people who read all the time. Their house was only four rooms for the parents and five kids. Their social conventions were completely different — quite an experience for me. They didn't flush the toilet; they fought about everything, right out front; and they were not concerned about changing their behavior in front of guests.

In each of our houses we had a picture of my great-grandfather Gary. He was quoted as having said, "Do something for the city, the country, and the community in which you live." My parents, particularly my mother, held high these values from early in my life. She worked with the Boys' Club of New York for 35 years; she helped the American Cancer Society raise a million dollars for hospitals; she supported the arts. If you were to ask her what has motivated her to do what she's done, she'd say, "I believe in doing something for the community that you live in."

My experience was different from a lot of kids I knew, in that my parents took it upon themselves to prepare me to follow this tradition of philanthropy and community involvement. When I was given my first quarter at age six, there was a definite ceremony about what it meant to have money. From the time of that first allowance my mother showed me how to keep records and open a checking account. She took me to Wall Street when I was nine, taught me basic economics when I was 11, and taught me some bookkeeping when I was 12. These moments stand out much more profoundly than any discussions she may have had with me about sex or any other momentous things one talks about with one's child.

Although my parents taught me a lot about money, I never heard them talk about their own finances at all, and I never saw them pay a bill or display any concern for the value of anything. So I always assumed my money too would be unending. This notion was proven true when my parents told me, at age 14, that I was going to inherit when I was 21. "You will have a trust and you'll never have to work again. It will give you many, many choices and enormous flexibility."

*   *   *   *   *

One of the most powerful experiences of my whole life came at age 18, at Sarah Lawrence College in my first theater class. We were instructed to do an exercise in which we were to sit next to another person and look into her eyes until we felt comfortable enough to pick up her hand. I sat opposite a Black woman who was about 19, and within two minutes I reached for her hand. She looked at me angrily and said, "I am *not* your nanny." I was floored. I realized that I had a lot of assumptions about myself and my experiences, and I had to look harder at myself.

I began to work on my assumptions about race and class, and sat in on meetings discussing the needs of people of color on campus. I leafletted and protested and did everything I could to push for their rights. While I felt completely out of place as a white wealthy person, I was nonetheless very open to telling about my class background and learning how different my experience was from others. I still didn't quite understand just how different other people's lives were, but it was the beginning of self-discovery, and of listening to and collaborating with people of color who were my peers.

*   *   *   *   *

A few months before my 21st birthday I took a class on money management. I was scared—the minute I got into it I realized how much I didn't know. However, I was motivated to learn by how incredibly patronizing my trust officer was to me, how he invariably addressed the answers — to my questions — to my brother. I was determined to know how to get proper attention.

Despite my fear of knowing too little, I began to plan. I asked my mother's attorney to explain the family trust and about the money I would receive. I found out that when I reached 21 I would get the income accumulated since I was 14, and realized that this income alone would be more money than I was ever going to need. Moreover, I'd get another chunk when I was 25, and again when I was 30, 35, and 40. It was clear to me that I could afford to give some of it away.

When I got my second trust payment at 25, I decided to give away half of whatever I got. I also decided that I needn't be limited to that, and that I could always make more money if I felt I needed it. Although I didn't feel the money was "bad" money, I recognized that it was earned off the backs of other people who worked very, very hard. Workers in companies got very little of the profits which came, in great part, from all their work. By giving principal, I chose to give much of it back.

*   *   *   *   *

Over the years the money grew, and I gave between $100,000 and $180,000 a year for over 14 years, about two-thirds of what I controlled apart from my home. I feel sure that I will always be committed to giving as much time and money as I can afford throughout my life.

I'm shocked by hearing how many women and men feel badly about having money and therefore just sit on it. Many have some jerk investing it in companies that have nothing to do with their values, while watching the government eat up millions of it in tax dollars. When we listen to our values, most of us have a great desire to do something very positive with our money. But we first need to break through our isolation and know we're not alone. When we have role models, then we can think bigger about what to do and how to get support for taking steps.

Over the years, I have made a number of loans to individuals and to social change projects. As a consequence, I've spent lots of time dealing with borrowers who do not pay back loans. I have not in the least enjoyed going after people, or having people run away from me on the streets when they see me because they know they owe me money. Now when I make a loan, the borrower and I each put aside a sum of money which, if they get into trouble paying back the loan, they use to hire a financial consultant. It's an insurance policy. It's also saying, "I want to invest in the success of this venture for you and at the same time, I don't want to be put into a situation where I've become identified as the Bank of America."

I've also hired a woman to manage the loans who follows up immediately when someone is late paying back. I've learned that assertive communication is an important part of making the commitment to a loan. I've learned repeatedly not to assume that people are proficient around money. Meeting someone halfway means sharing as much knowledge as possible about how to manage money.

*   *   *   *   *

Most people, if they looked at my financial situation, would say, "You're wealthy; you'll never have to think much about money!" However, if you grew up in a family which had an appetite for spending a million dollars a year and you had what I have now, you might feel like it was not quite enough. I sat down with someone and figured out that, given my living expenses, I would have to cut back my level of giving from $125,000 a year down to $40,000 a year.

As I see my principal dwindle sometimes I worry that I'm going to wind up one of the majority of older poor women in this country who live on less than $6,000 a year. Another part of me knows that I'm fine, mainly because I have experience working. For example, from age 22 to 25, I worked as an employment counselor helping progressive people find jobs with non-profits, and made $30,000 to $40,000 a year. I loved the work and may one day return to it. I'm an entrepreneur by instinct, and it's always been very easy for me to make money when I put my mind to it.

I pay my basic expenses such as food and shelter from my trust income. I justify this because I see myself as shepherding this money, and having my basic expenses covered enables me to do the work of getting the money back out to the communities. For the other half of my budget—more luxury expenses, such as entertainment and travel—I can't justify using the trust income: to entertain the shepherd with trips to Palm Springs doesn't seem appropriate. So I earn the money I spend on those lifestyle choices.

I own a small house and enjoy living there. I bought it for $100,000, and now after 12 years it's worth $900,000. I'd like to add a second story to it, but it just doesn't feel right to spend $100,000 in that way.

Many women I work with in the Managing Inherited Wealth group are just starting to realize their own abilities. If they don't have enough money to give away principal without jeopardizing their livelihood, I certainly don't advise it. I encourage people to develop their earning abilities. Earning gives you something: you look at that first paycheck differently than money that you haven't made.

I love the fact that I can stand on my own, able to earn money through hard work. On the other hand, this society has idealized independence, particularly in upper income families. It is important to acknowledge that we are all interdependent. What we do here, and what we do in Central America, and what someone does in the Middle East, all affect the global ecology, economy, and humanity. What goes on inside our hearts powerfully affects others. We are dependent on each other. I value this. Without doubt, one of the greatest benefits of having money has been the diversity of experiences it has given me. Not only have I been able to afford therapy to heal and grow, but I've learned about intimacy, connection and caring from my non-profit work. I acknowledge that I am dependent many times over in healthy ways— with my lover, with my good friends, and with my co-workers. These relationships sustain my mental health. If we live as isolated people, unable to build relationships, engrossed with our money, we will not be able to collaborate as we must to save and develop this planet—let alone our souls.

*   *   *   *   *

Many donors believe that simply by reading a newspaper or grant appeal we can understand what the community needs, when most of us have never been to the other side of the tracks. Most have never even had friends among the people we want to support, or even have talked with people different from ourselves about their visions for change.

That is why I prefer group decision-making with the involvement of folks from the populations that will be supported, to redistribute the power of money in terms of the decision-making process itself, and to counter my own tendency toward class arrogance. I'm always amazed at how much I learn from other people in this kind of group decision process. Of course, in collective decision-making the group needs to be chosen carefully from a diverse set of communities and experiences, and if we are going to bridge our differences, we need to listen respectfully to each other's experiences and digest them, not just react.

In the process of making challenging decisions with others, I have learned to consider other people. My experience is as important as theirs, but having more money does not give me any more weight in the decisions. Although money is an important resource and I happen to bring it to the table, we must all be recognized for our individual resources and contributions.

I don't give all my money through community institutions — I gain a lot by working at my own philanthropy. However, I'm careful to strike a balance between using my privilege to make decisions about helping others, and sharing that privilege with others. I now do half of my funding myself, and share decision-making about half of my funding with others.

*   *   *   *   *

I played a key role in starting The Women's Building and the National Network of Women's Funds. In the first four years, hundreds of thousands of dollars came in and thousands of people joined each organization. Because I was independently wealthy and we were trying to redistribute power and money, I was not given an official staff or board position. That was fine but unfortunately, I was also never given much support for my work, and I was targeted as a person with too much power. It was painful. From this experience I learned that we need to learn how to support leadership in our organizations and how to redistribute power without alienating anyone, rich or poor.

*   *   *   *   *

I get great satisfaction giving money and helping people raise money for their projects. It's about building dreams, building trust, about building relationships. I give from the heart and not just because I should. I rarely give from a sense of guilt—I give much more from feeling inspired. To help another person take one step closer to life, liberty and pursuit of happiness is incredibly rewarding.

When I was involved with the Vanguard Public Foundation, I saw that the amount of money I could give was a drop in the bucket, so I started calling up other people, foundations or corporations, to give money as well. I rarely give money to a project that I don't try to help with other fundraising or by offering technical assistance. In general my commitments to projects are long term. When my involvement works well, I help give a project skills and contacts, hope, confidence, and human connection. My work at The Women's Foundation, for instance, has fulfilled a lot of my dreams. Seventy-five other people are now taking leadership there, so I'm freed up to work on the national level helping to develop the newer women's funds. Frankly, my time is far more valuable for the community than the money I give.

I've been humbled in the last couple of years to understand how limited my time is, so now I budget time as well as money every year. Once a year in late January, I rent a house up in Lake Tahoe where I retreat alone. I look back at the previous year and think about where I've put my time and energy. I fill out forms in an elaborate evaluation process. I look carefully at how I feel about my work and how successful the strategy was. Then I examine what issues need to be dealt with that other people aren't adequately addressing right now. Mostly I meditate, give thanks, and pray for guidance and world peace.

Over the 15 years of my work, I would guess I've worked with over 1,000 projects. I feel enormous gratitude for I what have shared with people in those years. I feel touched that people within the women's movement took the risk to hold me accountable and tell me honestly, in spite of my privilege and position, what they really thought of me and my style—like how upsetting it was that I was constantly late, or what stood in the way of my being an effective co-worker.

What you can afford to do is not just a matter of counting what's in your wallet. It's basically about your willingness to take risks, about what's most important to you and about what kind of contribution you want to make. I feel hopeful for the future as I see more and more wealthy people using their money to make a difference in the world. Donors, particularly women, are taking more responsibility for their money and giving it away in powerful ways. We affect each other profoundly when we keep our hearts and our souls open rather than closing down and believing that nothing can happen. We are much stronger when we have role models and we know we are not alone.

My connection to a community of people committed to acting for social change has given me a precious gift: greater awareness of myself, of community, and of the world. When other people remark how much I am giving, I feel how much I have received and how inspired I am. My soul is fed, day in and day out.

PHIL VILLERS

Phil is a successful entrepreneur who developed three computer companies, and gave away half his wealth to create a foundation supporting advocacy for the elderly.

I came to this country as a refugee when I was five, having fled France with my family two hours ahead of the German Army. That may be one of the factors that gave me a strong social conscience from a very young age.

Our family did not have much money while I was growing up, but it was adequate for our needs. In high school I was widely viewed as the local radical. I was interested in studying cooperatives and socialism and had a different view of government than was common.

I was very unpopular in school, since being a non-conformist is not a highly prized virtue among children. My successes were mostly intellectual and I was therefore more appreciated by older people than by my peers. I got into a number of fights in school and got the worst end of the deal a number of times, particularly since when called upon to surrender, I just plain refused!

My father pushed me towards the sciences and engineering, and I decided to become a mechanical engineer. When I was a junior at Harvard, a classmate and I decided someday we'd start a company. Eventually we both did, but not with each other.

The start of my first company traces back to the early spring of 1968, when Martin Luther King was assassinated. The following week, a minister in my town preached a very powerful sermon, and it struck me that Martin Luther King had been only a few years older than I was, and that if I were really serious about making the kind of major contribution to social progress that I wanted, it was time for me to start.

So I sat down that very afternoon and drew up some alternatives. I considered changing careers to something more directly oriented to social change. However, I had neither a lot of money nor much experience or training in areas other than engineering. I concluded that the best method for me was to start a company and gain influence and money. In this society, one great source of influence is to be successful in business, both because of the success itself and because of the money it generates.

When I started my first company, Computervision, I had no top management experience. I decided to find somebody very experienced who would be the president, while I would act as senior vice president. I picked one of my old bosses, and he accepted. It was very clear that he was in charge.

One day the police came to arrest — for car theft — a young apprentice machinist who worked with us. A couple of hours later, my boss called me in and insisted that I fire him, because, whether he was guilty or innocent, the incident would "look bad." I refused and said that if the man was fired that I would have to resign. The young machinist stayed.

Having someone else as president in my first company was probably key to its success. However, after ten years, he and I were poles apart philosophically. So I left.

The second company I started, Automatix, developed robotics and artificial vision systems. The third business, Cognition, in a fairly new field called mechanical computer-aided engineering, produced software tools that allow engineers to create better products and designs.

I have liked the challenges and responsibility of business; I like being able to use authority to do what I feel is ethically right. The Nazis taught me that it is dangerous for business people to separate their private morality from their business morality. Separating those two moralities is anathema to me — I've worked to bring my social concerns into my business life. For instance, I've seen to it that none of the three computer companies I started have ever done any business with South Africa. All the companies I've started have had universal stock ownership, and when they became profitable, universal profit- sharing. I've promoted the concept of an open company, where people are free to talk to each other without going through a chain of command. I've opposed "executive perks" because I think they are highly divisive.

At the end of ten years in business I asked myself, "OK, you've become a successful entrepreneur, now what are you going to do for the world?" Again, I seriously considered a career change and agonized about it for the better part of a year. I finally decided to continue in business doing what I felt I was good at, while making a social change contribution through others, as an initiator and funder.

After wondering where to make a contribution, I decided that I wanted to make a change in the quality of the lives of elders. I picked this area the way I'm trained to, as an engineer: I compared and analyzed many options. I decided I wanted something that could really make a difference during my lifetime. Also, in the field of aging there was a particular advantage, in that I would not always be looked at as an outsider trying to do good — some day I too would be an elder. In addition, I have a lifelong dislike for waste in almost any form. I'm very conscious of the ways we waste human beings, essentially throwing older people on a scrap heap.

In 1981, my wife, Kate, and I held a series of brainstorming sessions in the living room of my home with an eclectic group of people. All were people I knew directly or indirectly, who I thought would be good resources to the project. We decided that the best way to exert influence on elder issues was by establishing a foundation which would both take an active role in the field and fund projects initiated by others. We met once a week to develop the idea and discuss its implementation. We discussed the mission, the priority areas, the methodology, what to spend on staff, how to identify projects we wanted to fund, how to evaluate effectiveness, and how long to continue the foundation.

By this time Computervision's value had gone up enormously. My entire fortune in stock was $80 million. I committed $40 million. I chose to give half because I didn't want to put all my eggs in one basket, yet I wanted to give enough to be able to have a significant effect. The only question was what was a major portion; 50% felt major.

One of life's realities is that many people who set a goal for themselves get lost along the way. By the time they have the means to realize their goal, they no longer care about it. Traditionally as people get older and build wealth and prominence, they move politically to the right, so I've always put myself forward as a candidate for a study on arrested development, because I haven't changed. I gave the $40 million to start the Villers Foundation because that is why I made the fortune in the first place.

I wrestled with how I could use wealth as a tool of influence without seeming to flaunt it. It seemed like a contradiction, and I had to make compromises. For example, I thought about whether to use our name in the foundation and decided there were more reasons for it than against it. Among other things, it helps make Kate and me more influential in the larger community, and that influence can be put to good use for the same goals as the foundation itself. My position in the Villers Foundation has been the equivalent of Chairman of the Board. I'm a fairly active president, but not the executive director — I play no role in the day to day management. I very purposely abdicated my right to make all decisions, and have been very pleased with the results. At first people had questions about my role, but the composition of the board answered that. The board members are very well known in their own right, and nobody would expect them to be somebody's patsy. I have had the satisfaction of working with a lot of very fine people — for instance, our former senator Paul Tsongas and congressman Barney Frank have both served on the board.

Probably the most important accomplishment of the foundation to date was helping create and fund an increasingly influential network of elder organizations, the Massachusetts Health Care Alliance. The Alliance led to the "Health Care For All" campaign and to the first state law in the country for universal health care.

Another significant accomplishment was changing the law about spousal impoverishment. It used to be if one spouse became disabled and had to go into a nursing home, then the second spouse had to spend down to a poverty level before the federal government would help with Medicaid. The only way around that was divorce! Reform measures liberalized the amount of income and assets that can be kept by the non-disabled spouse.

Outside the foundation, the area I'd most like to make contributions is human rights. I've been very involved with trying to end U.S. intervention in Central America. I'm a member of Baron's Business Executives for National Security, an organization of business people who do not think that true national security is enhanced by putting more holes in the ground with missiles in them. I've been active with the ACLU, and with Amnesty International. As I see it, they are all part of a coherent whole.

One of the most gratifying things I've done has been helping to free political prisoners. Probably my greatest satisfaction of all came from a trip to El Salvador about five years ago, on a fact-finding trip sponsored by the Unitarian Universalist Service Committee. On the plane, a woman who was involved with America's Watch told us a terrible story about a young woman doctor. She was treating refugees in the Archbishop of El Salvador's refugee center, when she and her husband were picked up by the national police. Their two-year-old twins were also taken, and the national police had refused to release the twins to their grandparents.

When we arrived in El Salvador, we made it our business to try and do something for this family. Everywhere we went we inquired, but we didn't find out much. We finally tried a bluff, at a prison right outside San Salvador. We asked to see the husband—and lo and behold he was there! We got to talk with him. He confirmed that they would not release the kids to the grandparents. He'd been tortured and his wife was in one of the women's prisons. The other half of our fact-finding group went to see her, and learned that her jailers had threatened to cut off her children's hands if she didn't support their claim that arms were being kept in the refugee center.

Two days later we were scheduled to meet the president of El Salvador, so we asked our congressman Jim Shannon to ask the president to free the twins. Jim agreed, and even suggested that it would be wonderful if the twins were released before we left. It worked, and the grandparents were extremely grateful. They brought the twins to our hotel. Some journalists were there, and we thought it'd be a nice gesture to put one of the children on Jim Shannon's lap. But the moment they were taken out of the arms of their grandparents they were completely terrified! The parents were still in prison, and it took an organized letter-writing campaign for the better part of a year, using all the resources I could muster, to get them freed. But we finally succeeded.

Now you can say, "These were only four lives — how about the millions?" I'm sensitive to that. However, I believe I'm sensitive in both directions: To work only for individuals and ignore the large numbers would be a little naive, but to say that you care for humanity en masse and not for human beings singly is sheer hypocrisy too. And even though I've never met those parents since they got out of jail, that was one of the most gratifying experiences I've ever had in my human rights work.

*　　　*　　　*　　　*　　　*

One of my greatest fears when I first became wealthy was that it would have a big impact on the way we lived. Fortunately, neither my wife nor I enjoy extravagance and conspicuous consumption. We changed our lifestyle somewhat, but to this day there are many things we don't buy because we think they're too expensive. We've never had expensive cars — in fact I'd been a millionaire several times over before I bought my first new car. We both enjoy traveling, but we don't travel luxuriously — I have never bought a first class airplane ticket.

We didn't want our children to be aware of our large wealth until they were older, because we were concerned about the impact of our wealth on their values. I've seen the impact that wealth has on a lot of young people, robbing them of needing to do something with their lives, making them take pleasure in superficial things. For instance, this year my son went to a private school and he said a lot of students bragged about how their parents had a Mercedes or a BMW — those were the kinds of things that were valued. We have tried to pass on a very different value system, and conspicuous consumption doesn't fit.

We are leaving money to the children, but not too much. We're leaving an amount big enough to give them a major head start, and not so big that they could spend the rest of their lives without having to earn something.

*   *   *   *   *

Giving away substantial wealth has never been difficult for me. I've had no regrets about what I gave; that's what the money was for. It has been a part of the much more important context of how I've led my life. I only regret that I could not do even more. Many people don't give what they could; I think it's out of fear. Saying "I'm not really wealthy enough yet" is just an excuse. You have to start giving to feel comfortable doing it.

The main advice that I'd pass on to others would be to figure out what you really want to do, otherwise you waste time, effort and money. When we set up the foundation, the year spent hammering out the agenda, how we would proceed, and finding the right people to do the work was a year very well spent. You have to focus. You can't do everything, but that should never be an excuse for doing nothing. Decide what you're going to do, and do it.

I learned early in life that if you try, it's amazing how often you can succeed. I still call myself "a notorious head thumper" — I bang my head against the wall because I like the sound as the wall cracks! I've cracked a fair number of walls.

GEORGE PILLSBURY

Dozens of articles have been written about the "Pillsbury dough boy" giving away dough. George used his money and energy to help develop the Haymarket People's Fund and the network of social change community foundations known as The Funding Exchange. He is currently a fundraiser for the National Jobs with Peace Campaign.

I come from a philanthropic Republican family and learned at a young age that giving away money was a natural and respectable thing to do. My parents are active in raising money for various causes, although the money they give is relatively modest compared to their means. They do give a lot to the Republican Party and occasionally to Yale. While their political values could make them liberal Democrats, class is a powerful influence and their class position has made them vote Republican. My parents are committed to social action, but they certainly don't believe in giving away financial principal.

When I was 18, I imagined organizing people of my class to use their money for progressive social change. This occurred to me one day after a debutante party that was particularly extreme in its display of wealth, held at the top of the RCA building in New York. I remember silver everywhere, because the father of the debutante had made all his money in South African minerals. I didn't know much about South Africa, but I knew it was bad.

Before the party even started, I went into the bathroom and ripped the buckles off my Gucci shoes. That was really symbolic, because back in 1968 Gucci shoes were a status symbol for a rich person, and I was into clothes. When I came out of that party at 4 a.m. and hit the streets of New York, I wanted to be out organizing a picket line against the party, rather than being part of it.

I felt troubled that some of the people at the party were my friends, and I didn't want to separate myself from them. I grew up so thoroughly upper-class — all the right vacation places, the boarding schools — everything right out of a textbook. I don't have any ethnic identity; I'm not Jewish, or black, or gay, or a woman. The only group with which I really feel a kinship is my class. That's why it came to me to try to organize people of my class—so I could continue to connect with the group that I grew up with. That is the basis for a lot of the organizing I have done with upper-class contributors to social change.

In college I was involved in the anti-Vietnam War and student movements. When I was 21, six weeks after four young people were killed at Kent State University in 1970, I received $400,000. This was money left over from the accumulation of the Pillsbury flour fortune. My view was that this money rightfully should have been going to the employees of the Pillsbury Company over the years, but was skimmed off and ended up in trust funds for people like myself. I felt it was not my money.

Within a few years I gave away about $300,000, including large sums to *Seven Days Magazine* (which collapsed after a while because it was too grandly ambitious), to the Film Fund, and to the Nicaraguan Sandinistas when they were still in the hills fighting then-dictator Anastasio Somoza. One day I handed the Black Panthers a paper bag with a hundred dollars in cash in it.

While I didn't feel too dependent on the money, I was scared that giving away the principal would limit my future ability to give, and therefore people wouldn't like me any more. I was also scared of feeling ripped off, that I might later feel I made the wrong decision if the things I funded didn't work out well. However, I felt relieved, too; giving away the principal felt like unloading a burden.

Then I met Obie Benz, a young man with money who had just set up a community foundation in San Francisco called the Vanguard Public Foundation. I was inspired, and in 1973 six or seven of us pooled our money to start Haymarket, modelled after Vanguard. We all agreed that we didn't have the expertise to make funding decisions alone, that we didn't have the time or the desire to become full-time philanthropists, and that we believed in involving other people and sharing the power. So we went right to the all-community board model, and Haymarket has maintained that tradition ever since. When I started Haymarket I gave only $25,000. Only one person contributed more — a man who walked in and gave us a check for $50,000. After he left the office we were screaming with excitement.

Over time Haymarket developed a small staff: David Crocker and I who both worked as unpaid donors, another volunteer who worked part-time, and two paid staff people. At first, there was conflict, as all the issues of money, gender and power got fought out between the paid and the unpaid staff. We didn't know how to deal with it, and we tried to have "criticism/self-criticism" meetings, which sometimes helped and at other times just caused huge battles.

One really big issue was that David Crocker and I knew all these rich people and were able to organize them to support our pet political ideas, independent of the foundation. Other staff people were angry that we used foundation time and resources to involve donors in projects that probably wouldn't have been funded if the paid staff had been given a say in the matter. One example was the Film Fund, which our co-workers saw as draining money and time. It was completely the idea of David Crocker, Obie Benz and myself, yet we could go ahead because we knew all the wealthy people. This infuriated the other staff.

This controversy raised fundamental issues of accountability. We eventually agreed that we would not raise money for our own special projects from Haymarket donors, and that if we had an idea we would solicit donors only with the agreement and collaboration of the community foundations.

There is always a tension between people who feel they can take initiative and those who feel they are left to sustain and develop what's already there. At times donors take creative initiative, set up funds and other projects, but then since they're volunteers they go off when something else takes their interest. Paid staff, on the other hand, can't just take off to do some other project when they feel like it. I regret that I left Haymarket after only four years, and that during the last two years I was already getting involved with the Film Fund.

In 1979, I got involved with setting up The Funding Exchange, a network created to build connection and coordination among the progressive community funds throughout the United States. I helped The Funding Exchange start a donor-advised program called the National Community Fund, and helped produce the *Gift Giving Guide* and *Directory of Socially Responsible Investments*, the first two publications of The Funding Exchange.

We've never been entirely successful in getting our message understood by the media. They seem to be more interested in what is glamorous or neurotic about wealthy people, and less interested in our giving money away and our commitment to social change. The first big article published about conferences was a mess: the *Village Voice* wrote a piece about me in which they lied and used a false photograph of me. So we decided to try to put out our message ourselves. After The Funding Exchange published *Robin Hood was Right* in 1977, we hired a professional public- relations firm in New York City to help us publicize it. We appeared on TV stations, radio, in magazines and newspapers throughout the East Coast — even the *New York Times* did a big article, and then we appeared on the Phil Donahue Show. It was a big deal! Since then, media coverage has been trickling along every year. People keep rediscovering the alternative foundations as if they were a new thing.

Through the years, working with the funds has been a powerful way to deal with my class background. As rich people, we have been taught that we are special. But this specialness is not real; it's pretense. The only way you can maintain it is by always putting people down: putting the middle class down, putting the lower class down, putting working people down, treating other people as if they were not real because they don't have what you have. Working with other staff and board members has enabled me to interact with all different kinds of people, from very different class backgrounds. It has taught me to be more genuine.

*　　　*　　　*　　　*　　　*

I got involved in setting up a community fund because it seemed like the most effective way to fund and model social change. I believe in the fundamental importance of grass-roots social change. The large social movements which make history, like the civil rights movement, the women's movement, and the environmental movement, gained their strength from small, local, grassroots organizations. For instance, in the case of the environment, the issue which started as a little Love Canal story 15 years ago resulted in the $10 billion Superfund passed by Congress, a major victory for the anti-toxics movement. But that victory came originally out of grass-roots activism, and to this day the issue of toxins is still being fought on the local grassroots level. Few individual donors can possibly know about these small groups in the way a board of community activists can, a board that brings together people who are directly involved in grass-roots action.

Community funds also build people's skills, such as fund raising, project evaluation, grant-making, financial management, decision-making, and board management. Democracy does not happen automatically—it requires empowerment and skill-building in people who don't have power. In other words, the only way to make democracy work is for people who do not have power to get power and to develop the skills to exercise it. One way that, as philanthropists, we can be truly philanthropic is to encourage people without power to take power. A fundamental intent of the community funds is to give people the power and skills to make funding decisions.

*   *   *   *   *

There is a continuum from having complete stewardship of one's money to total divestment. I would like to be at the total divestment end of the continuum, but, in reality, I'm in between. It is going to be hard for me in this lifetime to give away all of my money—there is just too much of it! Over the past three years my portfolio value doubled from $700,000 to $1.4 million. And just last year, at 37, I gained control over more money in another trust fund. There's more money coming—however, it might not come for many years, until after the death of my parents. I plan to keep chipping away at my extra wealth. Mary and I have agreed to set aside $500,000 to keep for ourselves. We aim to keep it at that level without increasing it.

Having children has made me more worried about money, more reluctant to give it all away. Part of my hesitation has to do with my relationship with Mary, who is from a different class background and is more reluctant to give away principal, although we do it anyway. Mary and I have few conflicts about money, though. We both prefer public school for the kids. We agree we'll give our children some inheritance, but we want them to have the experience of working for a living. We don't want security coming too much from the money they have inherited. We also don't want our relationship to be too mixed up with money, but rather focussed on family.

I'd like to rely more just on my salary than I do now, but I worry about whether I could earn enough money. It would be easier if I were a lawyer or had a vocation where I might make $30,000 or $40,000 or more a year, but it's more important for me to work for social change. At Jobs with Peace, I earn $20,000. I suppose I could ask for a raise; I find that $20,000 is not very much in this city. But then again, I have no idea where my expenses begin and my contributions end. There are a lot of costs I don't ask Jobs with Peace to reimburse. It's much easier not to do it. If we had to live on my income, I'd have to keep track of these things. I'd have to be more accountable to the real world, like everyone else. A small example is that it doesn't matter to me if I get parking tickets. But when I park in front of a bus stop that old women may have to walk around my car, buses can't stop there—which is somewhat anti-social. I don't think people should have that kind of privilege.

At the same time the principal provides a feeling of security. It's hard to imagine choosing to give up all the freedoms that I have right now, including economic security — the U.S. offers us precious little of it! Other freedoms include having a choice of jobs not dependent on salary; having the power to decide what to give money to; not having to keep careful track of money. Losing these would be difficult. The hardest things for me to give up would be the opportunity to travel and the ability to donate money.

I have many friends who don't need much money, so I wonder whether I really need it. Sometimes I would really like to experience living without privilege. I will probably give more when I get more support for doing it, especially the support of seeing others give principal, too. I find it reassuring that others who gave away a lot of their money are doing okay. We need more examples of people giving away principal. It's funny how little we, with all our progressive values, are redistributing wealth and power!

I feel that I wasn't very clear at the time I gave away substantial principal; now I would make a much more carefully planned decision. That's why I question whether people in their 20s and 30s should give away all their money — it takes years to find priorities in life, and having a family can influence your choices. However, I encourage people who *can* to give away all their unearned income at least. I also believe that people should give away *at least* enough principal so that their portfolio value does not increase above the rate of inflation.

If people are contemplating giving away money, I hope they will give to make a long-term difference — to build organizations, or to help create lasting change. I also caution against giving more than $50,000 to $100,000 to one group—unless it's an endowment. The morale boost of the gift is not necessarily related to the amount; groups are encouraged even when they receive small contributions.

The time is right—some people are getting sick of all of this money. The era of decadence is wearing thin. I think this mini-movement of people giving away significant privilege is a great example. It shows what is possible.

RAM DASS

Ram Dass was born Richard Alpert. While a psychology professor at Harvard in the 1960s, he became famous when he and Timothy Leary experimented with altered states of consciousness using LSD. Later, he sought a truly enlightened person whose consciousness would not be affected by taking LSD. He finally did find such a person, a guru with whom he studied in India. There he took the name Ram Dass, which means "servant of God." Ram Dass returned to the United States, wrote several books (including How Can I Help?) *and travelled extensively to talk about the relevance of a spiritual life. A few months before this interview, Ram Dass' father died living him an inheritance.*

My father made his money as a lawyer in Boston. My mother came from a relatively wealthy family, and she pushed my father into fundraising for the community instead of just making money. My father got increasingly involved in different philanthropies, including becoming president of the Board of Brandeis University and even of the New Haven Railroad. For a Jewish person to be a head of a railroad was a big deal. He raised money using religious identity and guilt. As a child, I sat through a great many fundraising meetings of the United Jewish Appeal.

From way back I wouldn't accept dad's money. I knew that he saw everybody as wanting his money, and I didn't want to be one of those people. It would mean that he wouldn't trust my love — it would seem conditional on his money. The few times I borrowed from him, I paid him back to the nickel.

I always had the idea that I could afford to be a flake — I could afford to get thrown out of Harvard and be wild because one of these days I was going to inherit a lot of money. Then one day when I was in India, my spiritual teacher Maharaji called me in and said, "Your father has a lot of money...You are not to accept an inheritance." I was startled. I said, "Okay," while thinking to myself, "I'll deal with that when the time comes." I didn't know whether I would honor what my guru said or not. I figured that coming from a family of lawyers I'd figure out a way around it. Yet, on a spiritual level his mandate felt right to me.

Once I shifted my intention towards my inheritance the effect was profound. No longer was my lifestyle impeded by my father continuing to live. I hadn't been aware that I was wanting his money and waiting for him to die. Now that I stopped doing so, suddenly I was helping him remarry, and he and his wife and I became close buddies. I just wanted him to be happy; he had worked hard, I wanted him to enjoy spending his money. Once I stopped wanting his money, I was freed up to love him — and he recognized that.

I knew that Dad had made his money as a Jewish, middle-class, responsible family man with the justification that he would pass it on and his kids would be secure. I knew he would feel rejected if I told him I had decided not to accept the inheritance, so I never spoke to him about it. Still, he must have picked up that I felt more relaxed towards him and his money, because he trusted me enough to name me executor of his will, passing over my older brother who is a lawyer. And when I said, "Dad, your signature is not being accepted any more, would you trust me with power of attorney?" He said, "Of course."

After Dad died I discovered that I was named as the sole beneficiary to an annuity that wasn't in the will. When I sat down with my brother Billy and the lawyer to go over the will I said, "I think Dad wanted us both to have the same amounts, so I'm planning to give you half of the annuity." Billy was very uncomfortable. "Well, we'll see about the gift tax," was all he said. If I hadn't done this it would have created an irreversible family rift. In some families, money is more powerful than blood.

In his will Dad left money outright to Billy. To my middle brother who is mentally disturbed he left an annuity which pays him weekly to cover what he lives on. But because I was into drugs and gurus, he left me installments over ten years, so I wouldn't blow it all at once. Four years before he died he asked me, "Do you want me to get rid of that clause?" I didn't care, so I told him, "Do what *you* want." He said, "We'll leave it. You never know how crazy you are going to be."

When my guru told me not to accept my inheritance, I set up a special account, into which all of the inheritance has gone and every penny will be given away. It was about $200,000 from the will and $100,000 from the annuity. I have yet to decide how to distribute most of the money.

*   *   *   *   *

I don't live like most people live. I'm involved in a sect called the Sadu, the wandering holy people. One winter, when I had settled into a little hotel up in the Himalayas with my heater and books and sleeping bag, all set up for a nice comfy winter of study, I got a message from my guru: "Ram Dass should go. He should not stay in one place so long. Water, if it stays in one place too long, turns bad. He can come back, but he should keep moving. Attachments develop." The next day I was gone. For 25 years I have been on the road nine to ten months a year, staying in a lot of people's homes. I've stayed in everything from "You can throw your sleeping bag in the corner" to a bedroom specially set up for me with flowers and silks. And in many many hotels — all are fine.

Once I checked into a hotel in Topeka, a typical plastic Ramada Inn. I set up my holy pictures and incense and thought, "Gee, a few more weeks and I can go home." I have a base camp I call "home," where my mail comes through and I check in. Then I thought, "Isn't this absurd; I'm always thinking of where I am in relation to this place I'm calling home. I've got to let go." So I went back out of the room, locked the door, opened the door again and yelled "I'm home!" Since then wherever I am is home.

It's hard to assess how much I live on in a year because when I'm on tour I simply pay my expenses and nothing comes through as salary. It looks like I'm making nothing, although, with all the airfares, hotels, and meals I'm probably living on between $20,000 to $30,000 a year. Last year I was 4-1/2 months on the road, went to 60 cities, and raised $800,000. I gave it all away. Previous years I've raised and given away between $125,000–$500,000.

In 1973 I started the Hanuman Foundation so that I could give the money I was earning to projects without personal tax. The Foundation has provided money to help start the Prison Ashram Project and the Dying Project, among many other things.

I give impulsively and love doing it. The other night I was down in New York at the Emmaus House, where five brothers and fifty-five homeless people live together as a community. They had a music group I saw perform at a church in Harlem. These ten homeless people with a little electric piano were doing jazz gospel, and they were really out there. They were still homeless people, but the music took them and their audience beyond their situation. I thought, "My god, this is something very powerful and pure." So I pulled out my checkbook and wrote a check for $500. I also loan a lot of people money and never charge interest. I often forget I loaned the money.

*　　　*　　　*　　　*　　　*

One day, a few people whom I knew through our guru Maharaji invited me to a meeting. They were setting up a foundation, called Seva. Most of the people at that meeting were members of the World Health Organization (WHO) and had big reputations. A Swiss woman, who was a doctor who had headed the Southeast Asia program for WHO, said, "We've wiped out smallpox. Now let's take on blindness! Research has shown that most blindness is preventable and curable in the world — let's just take it on and eliminate it!" I felt intimidated, a little boy playing this nickel-and-dime game while here was this big game. I just said, "Fine, sure, wonderful."

You see, since I was thrown out of Harvard in the '60s because of my drug and sexual identities, I've been a non-person in the established society. I've worked with prisoners and dying people because those are people the society is also forgetting about. Finding myself in Seva with all these "legitimate" people was baffling to me. For a number of years I helped Seva raise money, and then I became chair of the board. Suddenly I was part of a legitimate non-governmental organization and I was chair of the board! I was Dr. Dass with my tie and blue blazer bargaining with ministers of health for hospitals and clinics and setting up a medical school. My god, I never even got into medical school! My father would have been proud of me!

When I first became chair I tried to act unilaterally: I had gone to Guatemala and my heart opened. I said to people there, "You need more of this — of course we'll cover that." Within a day, I'd given away an extra $10,000. I came back to Seva and the executive committee said, "It's not in our budget." "I said, 'Well, I'll raise it!'" They said, "Sorry, that's not the point!" I felt a wrenching frustration. "What do I need this for," I thought to myself. "I think it should be done my way!" But over time I saw that when you represent an organization, you can't play behind the scenes. I also came to admit that being with the other people in Seva was more gratifying than doing it alone. I had been so used to calling the shots it was a big surrender for me to share control. When I stopped resisting it, I could see that the collective wisdom of the people in Seva was far greater than my own.

In the past, when our group struggled about some topic, be it about blindness or Native Americans or Guatemalans, I would make very declarative statements, and everyone would wait for me to get done so we could get on with the real process of joint decisions. I began to appreciate the beauty of collaborative decision-making. I came to see that my personality distorts how I hear truth. Each of our hearts is colored by our own life experiences, and each of our hearts has just one piece of the truth, and I became richer for developing the trust in others' intuition rather than just trusting my own. I even started consulting others about how to use my time. I would ask the board, "I have the next nine months free — how do you want me to spend it? Should I meditate? Raise money? Administer?" Deciding with others about time and money has been a great experiment in surrender.

We learn in Seva how to give to others without taking their power. We are clear that money is not ours — we are merely responsible for the movement of that energy. Our challenge is to accept the responsibility of the role of givers in society without identifying with that role.

I am so enriched by contact with the people we give money to, it would be hard for me to hold rigid roles of giving and receiving. When I am with doctors bouncing in a jeep in Nepal and we're getting dysentery together, who is the giver and who is the receiver? When I was a therapist I saw everybody as a patient. In a similar way, if somebody is very beautiful, or very disfigured, or very rich, most of us can't see the human being because we have gotten lost in those symbols. To the extent I treat anybody in terms of their symbolic value I am of no use to them, because I reinforce the symbols and lose the human connection. We have to reach for the highest level of truth we are capable of between human beings.

We see Seva as great theater. By playing our roles lightly, it's easier for us to be ourselves. At board meetings, when a person starts talking about how serious this or that is, we put on Groucho Marx glasses to lighten things up. We are dealing with Guatemalan murders, Nepali blindness, Native American alcoholism, and things can get very heavy. Keeping a balance of humor and love and responsibility enables us to keep exquisitely close to the spirit.

It took time for trust to develop in Seva, and at times it was extremely bumpy. At one meeting, Nicole, who had been running the blindness project, was charging ahead like General Patton. I interrupted her and said, "Nicole, I think you're going about this wrong. How you do it is as important as that you do it." She said angrily, "Would you have somebody needlessly blind one extra day?" "There are worse things than being blind," I replied. She said furiously, "Well I don't know of them!" Tension vibrated through the room and in everyone's guts.

One cause of the tension was that the group brought together "Be-ers" like me who never did anything, and "Do-ers" who never "be-ed" anything, and we converged in head-on collision. It took years for Nicole to soften into her be-ing and for me to get off my ass and to get things done. Both of us have been incredibly enriched by each other.

When we start board meetings we ask ourselves what uncompleted personal business we have with any one in the group. Someone says, "You two had a business deal that didn't work, and the vibration between you makes it impossible for us to go on." And I say to someone, "I think your other worlds are pulling you, and you are not present with Seva. I think you ought to examine your involvement." It's like group encounter. Finding truth with each other is an essential given of our work. We spend the first three days in closed meeting just to get ourselves clear. I express what is wrong within my own life and others do too. Pretty soon I feel the support of the family and my heart is opening. I share my personal life. We all do. Nobody has secrets. We have kept investing the group with our lives.

I think a group acting to care about the world is the highest game people can play together. But if you are going to invest in a group, make your group living truths or the hell with it! Once a foundation of wealthy donors asked me for my honest opinion of their group. I said, "Why don't you really play the game? You are playing it like a diddly thing, no risk, no real investment in each other. You are still holding the control of your own money, mostly making your own decisions. But how exciting if you were to put sizable portions of your money into a pot and all share in the decisions. How exciting if you were to be really honest with each other and invest in each other!"

What's a real commitment to giving? If I am giving away $10,000 a year and I have a $1 million and am set for life, while 40 million children are dying, so what? If your child is hungry, you get food for the child. The question is who isn't your child? You have created boundaries in your heart — what has holding onto those boundaries cost you?

When you are quiet enough, you see that it is too great a cost to turn your eyes away from the disenfranchised in order to be happy. Yet I have watched how difficult it has been for me to shed my middle-class aversions to involvement with the immense suffering of the hungry, poor, politically tortured, sick, and dying in the world. By clinging to the affluence we enjoy in America, I was cutting myself off from acknowledging all people as my brothers and sisters. [1]

To the extent that we identify with money or with righteousness from giving it, we will be unhappy and insecure. The minute that we are not identified with having money or giving money, and are quiet enough to listen to the whole existential situation — including our own needs and what money can do and what it can't do — then constructive action will occur. You might not even understand it, but your intuitive heart will say yes, and you'll do something.

Don't be afraid of making mistakes. I make lots of mistakes — I've loaned money to people and they've ripped it off. I've given money and they've used it poorly. But that's their problem, not mine. I did it with a good heart and the best wisdom I had available. Taking risks is an exercise in learning to listen to yourself.

I suggest to people starting off in this game: keep what you need for your personal needs and family responsibilities. Then be a trustee for the rest of the money. Use it wisely. There is no rule book about that wisdom, no right or wrong. Nobody is better or worse. Pass the money through you as a way to heal the universe. Listen to what heals — have your life serve as your message. The way you live has to be the way you do it!

1. This paragraph quoted from an article by Ram Dass in the Fall 1987 Seva Foundation newsletter: *Spirit of Service*.

APPENDICES

Questions for Reflection and Discussion

Class Background Exercise and Class Spectrum Chart

Financial Timeline Exercise

Thumbnail Biographies

Annotated Bibliography

Resource List

Support for Making Change

QUESTIONS FOR REFLECTION AND DISCUSSION

We offer these questions to help you examine how the main themes of this book relate to your life. You could use the list in many ways: for example, alone, exploring your thoughts by thinking or writing; with a friend, by talking together about the questions you're both drawn to; informally, by starting a conversation over dinner with a thought-provoking question; or formally, by organizing a group to go step-by-step through the list. Don't limit yourself to this list—we hope you will come up with your own questions, based on your own situation.

Chapter 1: Giving It Away

1. If someone gave you $100,000 to give away, what would you do with it?
2. How do you decide how much to give? What do you like about how you give and how could you make it more fulfilling?
3. What do you consider necessities; what do you consider luxuries; and why? What surplus do you have and what are you doing with it?

Chapter 2: What's My Fair Share?

1. Do you see yourself as well-off, about average, or badly off? To whom do you compare yourself?
2. How do your income and assets compare to those of others nationally and globally? (Look at charts on pp. 31–33)
3. What were you taught about why some people were poor and others rich? What do you believe about where wealth comes from?

Chapter 3: Liberating the Rich

1. What is your class background? For a frame of reference, look at chart on pp. 166–167. For a more personal picture, do exercise on pp. 164–165.
2. What was good about your class background and what was difficult?
3. What limits were defined by your class background? How have they confined you and how have you transcended them?

Chapter 4: Finding Security

1. What are your images of security? What are the sources of security in your life right now?
2. What did you learn growing up about relying on others? On whom can you rely for emotional or financial support?
3. What kinds of fears and insecurities do you have about the world around you? Is there some social change work you could do that might improve the situations which give rise to those fears?

Chapter 5: Beyond Guilt and Shame

1. What do you feel proud about — and what do you feel shame or guilt about — in your relationship with money?
2. Are there ways that shame and guilt have been positive motivators in your life? If you feel guilty about money, how does your guilt motivate you? What might be better ways to motivate yourself?
3. How does your present way of living and handling money match your values? In what ways are they consistent with your values; in what ways are they not?

Chapter 6: Revealing Ourselves as Wealthy

1. Which of the following factors about disclosing your net worth and how you use money are important for you? Are there others you would add to this list?

Fears about Disclosure:
___Risk to sense of equality with co-workers, friends
___Stereotypes and judgments made about you
___Being asked for money
___Risk to certain roles — e.g., as activist or fundraiser
___Embarrassing your family
___Shame and guilt
___Fear of publicity
___Fear of harm — robbery or kidnapping

Benefits from Disclosure:
___Greater openness, honesty in relationships
___Ability to seek direct support
___Relief from pretense
___Recovering pride
___Reducing isolation
___Working for diversity of contacts
___Presenting a model for others of being honest about money
___Working against a status quo protected by secrecy
___Possibility of fascinating conversations

2. Think of one person with whom you might like to be more open about your money situation. How might you minimize the negative factors you checked above and build upon the positive factors?
3. Do you know any people with wealth who could use support about the issue of secrecy? What can you do to help them? What kind of support do you need yourself to be comfortable talking about how you relate to money?

Chapter 7: Families and Money

1. How did your parents handle money? Who made decisions about financial matters in your family? At what age were you involved, if at all?
2. How are your values and attitudes about money, lifestyle, and giving similar to or different from those of your partner? How do you work out differences?
3. How do you educate (or plan to educate) your children about money, spending, giving, lifestyle choices? If you plan to pass along assets to them, what are your hopes and fears about how wealth will affect their lives?

Chapter 8: Finding Meaningful Work

1. How does your financial situation affect your work choices? If you are self-employed, do you pay yourself a salary and try to live within a budget?
2. If you do not get paid for your work, how do you measure its value? How do you know when you are doing a good job? To whom are you accountable: for priorities and plans, for the results or productivity? How could you build both support and accountability into your work?
3. How has your past and present work fit into the four options presented (find a fulfilling career, fund your own work, make philanthropy your work, become a social entrepreneur)? What do you see as the pros and cons of your choices?

Chapter 9: Sharing Power and Privilege

1. What sorts of power and privilege has your money and class background brought you? Which might you share and how?
2. Do you involve others in your decisions to give away money? What portions do you give by each of the methods below?
Personal......Advisory......Collaborative......Community
3. What do you see as the pros and cons of sharing your giving decisions with others? Would you like to involve others more in your giving decisions? What holds you back? What would you need to move further?

Chapter 10: Spiritual Economics

1. What is your religious or spiritual heritage? What guidance does it offer about what kind of economic relationships to have with people? Which values of your heritage serve you; which no longer have meaning for you?

2. With what religious or spiritual community or practice are you currently involved, if any? What guidance do you receive about what kind of economic relationships to have with people? Which values of your current community serve you; which values do not speak to you?
3. What values underlie the day-to-day economic relationships you have with people? Where do you experience harmony between your values and practice and where do you experience gaps?

Chapter 11: Our Giving Makes a Difference

1. Have you experienced that your giving makes a difference? If yes, how, and if not, what motivates you to keep giving?
2. What doubts and concerns do you have about your giving? How could you resolve them?
3. Which of the ways suggested (in Chapter 11) to become more effective at giving are you already doing? Which would you like to try?

Chapter 12: Doing A Lot With a Little

1. What resources do you enjoy sharing with others? What resource(s) have you resisted sharing with others? Why? What would make it work for you to share those with others?
2. Who is a role model for you of someone using their resources to have an impact?
3. Which ways suggested (in Chapter 12) of doing a lot with a little do you already do? Which other suggestions interest you? What would enable you to actually do them?

A PICTURE OF
YOUR CLASS BACKGROUND

Class background consists of a large array of factors; it is often difficult or inaccurate to reduce these to a simple label. This exercise provides a more detailed picture of your class background, and may yield insights into yourself and the nuances of class. Fill in the following two pages with words that describe your past, present, and future situation.

	ANCESTRY	PARENTS/GUARDIANS

CULTURE/VALUES
  ethnicity
  race
  religion

FAMILY ATTITUDES
  about saving
    spending
    giving
    work

**EDUCATION/
WORK**
  type of schools
    education
  kinds of work
  status, pay

FINANCES
  income
  assets
  debts
  inheritance
  dependents

LIFESTYLE
  home
  neighborhood
  material comfort
  quality & type
    of material goods

OTHER
  (add your own)

	GROWING UP	ADULTHOOD	FUTURE PROSPECTS
CULTURE/VALUES			
ethnicity			
race			
religion			
FAMILY ATTITUDES			
about saving			
spending			
giving			
work			
EDUCATION/ WORK			
type of schools			
education			
kinds of work			
status, pay			
FINANCES			
income			
assets			
debts			
inheritance			
dependents			
LIFESTYLE			
home			
neighborhood			
material comfort			
quality & type			
of material goods			
OTHER			
(add your own)			

A SPECTRUM OF CURRENT CLASS GROUPS IN THE U.S.

Class is a hidden issue in the United States. Even though differences among people from various social and economic classes are part of our daily experience, class distinctions are seldom discussed openly. Distinctions in class are not simply financial: education, values, attitudes, race, and social standing are important parts of a complex puzzle. The puzzle is further complicated because financial factors may mix with cultural patterns in ways that seem contradictory: for example, upper middle-class Yankees fix things that many working class people throw out. People exploring issues of class and privilege have learned a lot from examining their own class backgrounds, and by contrasting their experience with those of others from other backgrounds. Explore in what ways the following brief descriptions of different classes fit you and people you know. You may not agree with the categorizations or the descriptions below — the spectrum is simply offered to stimulate your thinking.

Very Poor: They lack basic needs generation upon generation; most are undereducated, underemployed or unemployed.

Poor: They lack sufficient money to meet basic needs (e.g., health care, food, shelter, protective clothing). They repair and pass down clothing and household items. Many have dropped out of grade school or high school, and are unable to secure ongoing work. Many do not have bank accounts and cannot qualify for credit.

Working class: Their basic needs are usually met, but they have to save up for and choose between simple luxuries (e.g., eating out o̲r̲ getting a washing machine). Much of what they buy is second-hand or purchased on costly credit terms. In the past, few went to college; now many go to vocational school or to a community college. Their "blue" and "pink" collar jobs (e.g., cashier, clerical worker) now rarely provide sufficient earnings for families to buy their own homes, except in poor neighborhoods or with government help.

Middle class: Many go to college (often state schools) and go on to "white collar" jobs or become owners of small businesses. Many middle-class families buy modest homes, although this is becoming increasingly difficult even for families with two incomes. They can save up for luxuries (e.g., summer camp, a new car).

Upper-middle class: Most expect to (and do) go to private colleges. Homes are large enough so that every family member has a room, and many own a more modest second home. Luxuries are attainable without saving (e.g., travel abroad, new cars). Most have "professional" jobs. Many receive periodic money from parents and/or a five- or six-figure inheritance later in life.

Upper class: Many go to elite boarding schools, have several people paid to work in their homes (e.g., housekeepers, gardeners), and take a fair amount of luxury for granted. Most have assets sufficient to support their families without working. Children often take lucrative positions in family enterprises. Many receive a seven- or eight-figure inheritance both for themselves and for their children.

Ruling class: They not only have great wealth, but also considerable power. Most are from old upper-class families, and have been groomed from childhood to take positions of great influence in business, politics and/or the community. Many have great political influence behind the scenes.

Mixed class: A variety of combinations exist. Some examples: each parent is from a different class background; families have experienced a great change of fortune; people who have emigrated.

FINANCIAL TIMELINE

This exercise encourages you to define your current financial situation and project your finances into the future. By doing the work to clarify your needs in this way, you may discover ways to be more creative and flexible with your resources. Feel free to change the suggested time frame and money categories so they best fit your situation. If you have not already done so, you may find it useful to go through one of the various financial planning workbooks on the market and to consult a financial planner.

	present	in 10 years	at retirement

INCOME

-earned
-investment
Total

EXPENSES

Personal expenses
   (support for just yourself)
Living expenses
Insurance
Retirement savings
Self-development
   (eg. travel; classes)
Home improvements
Business development
Total

Money management
   expenses
Taxes
Investment management
   fees
Professional services
   (eg. legal)
Total

	present	in 10 years	at retirement

Community (support of people close to you)
Children
Partner
Mutual aid (to friends and allies)
Total

Social (support to a better world)
Social change giving
Sharing expenses with people with whom you share a common purpose
Total

ASSETS

Personal
Home
Portfolio
-children's fund
-cushion
-personal living expenses
-special projects
Total

Organizational
Foundation or donor-advised fund
Business

Future inheritance(s)
Likely
Possible

LIABILITIES

Home mortgage
Business financing
Consumer loans
Other debts
Total

THUMBNAIL BIOGRAPHIES

Through the course of this project we interviewed 40 people (or couples) who gave at least 20% of their assets and at least $100,000 to promote social change. Since only 16 could be featured in the book, we include here very brief profiles of the other people. (Some interviewees requested we not use their real names; their pseudonyms appear in quotation marks).

Jaime Babson: As a result of his travels in the Third World and the spiritual inspiration of people he encountered, including Gandhi's heir, Vinobha Bhave, Jamie decided to give away most of his inheritance. He wrote a check to every significant peace group he knew of in the U.S. He now devotes his time to peace work, living on income from a trust controlled by his family.

David Pillsbury Becker: A millionaire at age 21, David became an art collector and a museum curator. He has given college endowments for the arts, and helped produce socially-conscious films such as *The Life and Times of Harvey Milk*. He also supported Haymarket People's fund, with which he has been actively involved for many years. At age 42, David transferred a substantial portion of his assets to support an endowment drive at The Funding Exchange and to help establish a new national lesbian and gay fund.

Leslie Brockelbank: After many years of working as an activist, Leslie decided to give away half her capital to support social change projects in the Northwestern United States. She and her husband invited a group of 40 activists whom they knew and respected to devise a plan for distributing the money. In 1976, the group started a community foundation called the McKenzie River Gathering which raised additional funds, joined The Funding Exchange, and continues to fund progressive groups in the movement for social justice.

"Elizabeth C.": Born into a working class Scottish Presbyterian family, Elizabeth was a mother and housewife who lived a comfortable upper-middle-class life for many years. After her children were grown, she received a sizable inheritance and gave it away with the assistance of the Community Foundation of New Jersey. Over the years her money helped low-income groups — mostly African-American and Native-American — organize for housing and other basics of a decent life.

Robert Cabot: During World War II, Robert shocked his wealthy family by enlisting in the military as a private. After leaving the army he worked ten years for Marshall Plan agencies. He finally left his high-ranking government post because he believed the foreign aid program was exporting American materialism and inappropriate technology. "We were getting them to build big dams when they should be doing land reform." He moved to Italy and lived frugally for 20 years, writing novels. When he returned, he travelled across the U.S. for two years visiting spiritually-based intentional communities. For six years he has lived in a small rural commune in Canada, where he and his wife are both actively raising their young children. They fund U.S.– Soviet citizen diplomacy and land trusts for spiritual communities. Robert is 66 and taking a major role in raising his young sons.

"**Thomas, Dan and Barry Claggett**": Thomas is British, from an old Quaker family that made their wealth in shoes. He put most of his fortune into a charitable family trust which funds mostly peace and environmental concerns. He gave his four children only enough each to buy a house. However, this money appreciated over the years until it covered far more than their housing costs. When Thomas' sons Barry and Dan were in their 40s they joined their father in supporting the trust by each giving about 20% of his assets. Dan is an acupuncturist and Barry administers the trust.

"**Bill Cornfeld**": Bill's grandfather made a fortune selling toilet paper and napkins all along the east coast, and Bill grew up in affluence on Fifth Avenue in New York City. His family expected him to become a successful professional, but instead he went to live in a Zen Center when he graduated from college. During his five years there he met the woman he married and together they studied Buddhism in Japan. When he returned to the U.S. he helped launch the Nuclear Freeze campaign. Since then, with the help of a skillful friend and a sizable piece of his inheritance, Bill established a foundation which supports community-based peace organizations.

"**Mary Jane Donaldson**": Mary Jane grew up in a progressive family, with a tradition of family giving. After getting out of college, she joined a group of wealthy progressives, "Associated Rich Folk" and learned about The Funding Exchange. She gathered a board of activists and started a small fund in her own state. She gave that board $100,000, (20% of her assets), which was intended to fund its work until it could find other sources of support. After working in day-care and as a kindergarten teacher, Mary Jane visited the Findhorn Community in Scotland, traveled through South Africa and India, and then started a career in global education. She has served on the boards of "A Territory Resource," a collaborative donor fund in the Northwest, and is active with the Threshold Foundation.

Carol & Ping Ferry: Carol hired Ping, a foundation administrator, to assist her in running a foundation set up by her late husband. The team (who subsequently married) decided they wanted to give away the foundation's principal over five years. This they accomplished ($1 million a year). They prided themselves in responding immediately to requests for money, avoiding the slow, often bureaucratic, process of most foundations.

"**John Gaskell**": John's family's wealth came from a lumber company started by his great-grandfather. His first major conflict with his father came when he insisted on going to war as a private, not as an officer, to see what it was like for everyone else. John founded an alternative high school. He taught there for 30 years, and worked in the school desegregation movement. In addition to giving generously to alternative education, John also gave a large seed gift to help start the Haymarket People's Fund in Boston and set up a donor-advised fund for anti-war groups with the American Friends Service Committee. In all, he kept $1 million and gave away $1.5 million. At 64, John is retired and has a second family with young children.

"Elinor Goldfarb": Elinor grew up in a wealthy New York Jewish family. At an early age she was horrified by the contrast between the affluent and the poor which was so evident around her in the city. After traveling in Nicaragua, she studied community economic development. She has taken an active part in the alternative community development movement, by helping to develop a community loan fund and by encouraging The Funding Exchange network to invest their assets in community investments.

Paul DuPont Haible: After graduating from college in the late '60s, Paul received $1 million inheritance. He became active in opposition to the Vietnam War, and in the early '70s worked in prison rehabilitation. For many years he was a staff person at the Vanguard Public Foundation in San Francisco. He gave away roughly 25% of his principal, mostly to Vanguard Foundation and The Funding Exchange, with smaller contributions to Central America, Philippines and Native American solidarity work. Many other members of the DuPont family also fund social change.

Alan Bob Lans: Growing up in a liberal Jewish family, Alan was warned not to let people know he came from a wealthy background. Memory of the Holocaust and anticipation of future disaster had deeply affected his family's attitudes about money. During his late 20s, Alan worked through many fears about having and giving away money, and gradually became more open with friends and fellow social activists. He asked close friends from working class backgrounds to help him decide where to make contributions and over several years gave a total of one-third of his inheritance to Haymarket People's Fund and to gay and lesbian rights organizations.

Joan Martin: In 1984, guided by the Ministry of Money, Joan went on a pilgrimage to Haiti where she helped care for the poor. Powerfully moved by her experience, she reflected on the injustice of poverty and a new sense of what made her life rich. Determined to act on her realizations, she "invaded" the principal of her revocable trust and bought a building in a major east coast city, to be a medical temporary care facility for homeless men. She writes, "I have seen the Spirit at work and seen their lives as they are loved back to health by caring hands and hearts. I, in turn, have been loved back to a health and freedom I have never experienced before — by these very men. Co-creating with God has set me free."

"Richard Moulton": Richard started to depart from the views of his conservative family when he saw poverty first hand as a social worker. On trips to Guatemala and El Salvador, he observed the U.S. role in helping Central American governments suppress the people, and was inspired by the struggles of the people's movements to improve their living conditions. Over eight years he gave away almost all of his $250,000 inheritance to help the people in Central America. For many years Richard directed a major philanthropic institution and served on boards of other nonprofit organizations.

"Sam Murphy": When he was still in high school, Sam discovered that the Ku Klux Klan was becoming active in his county. He organized a vigil to counter these activities. In college, he was active in the university divestment campaign, in efforts to stop CIA recruiting on campus, and in promoting affirmative action. After college, Sam worked briefly on a farm and then got involved with an organization aimed at stopping U.S. intervention in El Salvador. With the $650,000 he received from the sale of his grandfather's farm, Sam set up the Green Mountain Fund to fund peace and social justice groups in Vermont. After instructing that the fund's entire principal be given away within ten years, Sam gave all control of the fund to an activist board. The board loans out the principal of the fund at no interest to groups meeting basic human needs, and as the loans are repaid the money is given away. Sam is in graduate school, aspiring to teach economics at the university level.

"Pierre Piran": Pierre grew up in a poor Black neighborhood in Jersey City. His father was a minister at what was called the "Slum Church." Although he was white, Pierre felt accepted by Black people. He identified with them, and developed an abiding allegiance to the Black liberation movement. Pierre felt that oppressed people who struggle for their own survival help all of us have a more democratic society. After college he lived in Washington D.C., in the midst of the '60s civil rights and anti-war activities. He gave away a portion of his wealth. Looking back, he would have given some of it more carefully: he is pleased with giving to the Catholic Worker movement and to American Indian organizations, but thinks that a few groups squandered the money he gave them. Pierre is now raising a family and writing novels.

Pratt Remmel Jr.: When Pratt was 20, he attended a public hearing investigating pollution of a large lake by a local utility company. He was the only one to stand up and testify against the utility — a company owned by Pratt's family. In the 20 years since, Pratt has used the income from his small fortune to support his work as a full-time volunteer environmentalist with a variety of organizations. He also serves on the board of the Peace Development Fund, which gives grants to grassroots peace groups. Pratt lives in Arkansas with his wife and daughter.

Sara Robbins: Sara started the Women's Solidarity Fund in 1983 in England. It funds projects empowering women, including rape crisis centers, battered women shelters, and sewing cooperatives in South Africa. Sara contributed the equivalent of $200,000 to the fund, the taxable limit for a trust that was not a recognized public charity. The fund includes lesbian and working class women on the Board. Sara has worked for Oxfam, and did voluntary service in Uganda in a district school.

Grace Ross: After finishing Harvard, Grace helped create an organization for low-income women called the Women's Alliance. Grace also trained hundreds of people in nonviolent action for the Pledge of Resistance campaign against U.S. intervention in Central America. She has been substantially involved in women's direct actions for peace and social justice, including an action at Wall Street called "Not in Our Name." After her mother's death, Grace called together a group of activists she respected (cross-class, race, and sexual orientation) and together they decided how to give away her $650,000 inheritance, with a focus on grants to groups of low-income women.

"Ned Stoner": Ned's father made a lot of money in real estate. At age 36, Ned received several hundred thousand dollars. He had been deeply involved for years with a global spiritual and social service organization, and was excited by a project the organization was sponsoring: converting land in a very poor area of India into a model development project run and owned by the local people. Ned gave money to this project and to support the organization. After going to several conferences for people with inherited wealth, and talking about his feelings about his family and security, Ned decided to give away almost all of his wealth. He organized a group of people from different class, cultural, and national backgrounds to decide what to do with the money. Ned is now raising a family, and remains happy with his giving decision.

Jacob von Uexkull: Jacob made his fortune in stamp collecting, and contributed 25% of his assets (amounting to the 1990 equivalent of $1 million) to start The Right Livelihood Foundation. This foundation awards an alternative to the Nobel prize to people who provide outstanding service to humanity, whose work is unrecognized by the mainstream. In his will, he committed 50% of his remaining net worth to the foundation. He was a Member of Parliament for the Green party in Germany, and is raising a family.

ANNOTATED BIBLIOGRAPHY

If you find the following bibliography and list of organizations useful, you may wish to send away for the complete 16-page spiral-bound resource list: **Taking Charge of Our Money, Our Values, and Our Lives,** *from which these were excerpted. It is available from the Impact Project for $8 postpaid.*

Albert, Michael and Robin Hahnel. *Looking Forward: Participatory Economics for the Twenty-first Century.* Boston: South End Press, 1991. Describes in convincing detail how participatory economics could work as an alternative to capitalism and communism. Filled with cartoons and quotes.

Benjamin, Medea and Andrea Freedman. *Bridging the Global Gap: A Handbook to Linking Citizens of the First and Third World.* Cabin John, MD: Seven Locks Press, 1989. A guidebook on how to support people in other parts of the world, including such methods as conscious travel, foreign aid, and alternative trade. Contains a 100-page resource directory.

Bodner, Joan, ed., *Taking Charge of Our Lives: Living Responsibly in the World.* San Francisco: Harper & Row, 1984. A guide to developing one's lifestyle with an awareness of global needs, including chapters on food, shelter, work, children, and health care.

Brouwer, Steve. *Sharing the Pie.* Carlisle, PA: Big Picture Books, 1989. A concise, easy-to-read picture book analyzing problems underlying the U.S. economy and why the gap between rich and poor is growing. Includes eye-catching tables and illustrations by the author. Available for $6 from Big Picture Books, P.O. Box 909, Carlisle, PA.

Center for Budget and Policy Priorities, "Drifting Apart." Washington, DC: CBPP, 1990. Documents the widening gap between rich and poor during the 1980s. Available for $4 from CBPP, 777 N. Capitol St., NE, Washington DC 20002.

Conn, Sarah; Tova Green; Nancy Moorehead; Anne Slepian; and Peter Woodrow. *Keeping Us Going: A Manual on Support Groups for Social Change Activists.* Cambridge, MA: Interhelp, 1986. A short manual on why and how to run an effective support group. Available for $6 from: Anne Slepian, 21 Linwood St., Arlington, MA 02174.

The Council on Economic Priorities. *Shopping for a Better World: A Quick and Easy Guide to Socially Responsible Supermarket Shopping.* New York:

Ballantine, 1991. A pocket-size guide which rates the producers of over 2000 brand name products on 11 social issues.

Domhoff, G. William. *Who Rules America Now?* Englewood Cliffs, NJ: Prentice Hall, 1983. An informative analysis of the upper class and the power structure of our society.

Dominguez, Joe. *Transforming Your Relationship with Money and Achieving Financial Independence*. A set of tapes guiding individuals towards how to secure enough money to live consciously and do fulfilling work without ever again worrying about a paycheck. All profits from the tapes are given away. Available for $60 postpaid from the New Road Map Foundation, P.O. Box 15981, Seattle, WA 98115.

Domini, Amy L.; Dennis Pearne; and Sharon L Rich. *The Challenges of Wealth: Mastering the Personal and Financial Conflicts*. Homewood, IL: Dow Jones-Irwin, 1988. A well-organized and anecdotal guide covering many aspects of how to come to terms with having wealth.

The Economist Book of Vital World Statistics. New York: Random House, 1990. A book of charts and graphs offering at-a-glance international comparisons on dozens of subjects including: income levels, standard of living, housing, health, population, industry, defense, environment and family life.

Ekins, Paul. *The Living Economy: A New Economics in the Making*. New York: Routledge & Kegan, 1986. An anthology of articles articulating a vision of economics "as if the environment and people really mattered."

Fischer, Louis, ed. *The Essential Gandhi*. New York: Random House, 1962. An anthology of selected writings by Mahatma Gandhi.

Gandhi, Mahatma. *Trusteeship*. Ahmedabad, India: Navagivan Publishing House, 1960. Describes Gandhi's philosophy about trusteeship of wealth.

The Giraffe Project. "The Giraffe Gazette." A quarterly newsletter, bursting with inspirational stories about ordinary people who stick their necks out for the common good. Subscriptions come with the $25/year membership (individual copies $3 each). The Giraffe Project, P.O. Box 759, Langley, WA 98260.

Goldberg, Jim. *Rich and Poor*. New York: Random House, 1985. Powerfully evocative photographs of rich and poor people in the U.S., including handwritten comments by each photo's subjects.

Hallowell, Edward M. and William J. Grace. *What Are You Worth?* New York: Weidenfeld & Nicolson, 1989. A stockbroker and psychiatrist offer financial advice for 17 personality types and suggest how to achieve emotional well-being in relationship to money.

Hollender, Jeffrey. *How to Make the World a Better Place: A Guide to Doing Good*. New York: Quill, 1990. A recipe-book of 124 different actions you can take to protect the environment, reduce global hunger, invest money responsibly and improve the world in other ways. An excellent resource.

Hyde, Lewis. *The Gift: Imagination and the Erotic Life of Property*. New York: Vintage, 1983. This richly creative study explores the act of giving, from tribal societies to ancient Western history to modern poets.

Independent Sector. *Giving and Volunteering in the United States*. Washington, DC: Independent Sector, 1988. A study of the motivations, attitudes and demographic characteristics of people who give and volunteer. Available for $27.50 from Independent Sector, 1828 L St. NW, Washington, DC 20036.

Institute for Community Economics (I.C.E.). *The Community Land Trust Handbook*. Emmaus, PA: Rodale Press, 1982. Land trusts enable homes to stay affordable, owner after owner. The book provides case studies and information on how to set up land trusts. Available for $7.50 (below retail price) from I.C.E., 57 School St., Springfield, MA 01105.

Levy, John. "Coping with Inherited Wealth." San Francisco, 1986. A short monograph cataloguing psychological problems of growing up with inherited wealth, including advice to wealthy parents. Available for $10 from John Levy, c/o Carl Jung Institute, 2040 Gough St., San Francisco, CA 94109.

Longacre, Doris Janzen. *Living More With Less*. Scottdale, PA: Herald Press, 1980. A Mennonite approach to a socially just, ecological and spiritual lifestyle, filled with practical suggestions contributed by hundreds of people from the U.S. and around the world.

McCamant, Kathryn and Charles Durrett. *Cohousing*. Berkeley: Ten Speed Press, 1989. Cohousing is a planned community model that offers participants a nurturing and practical balance between community and autonomy. The book describes how cohousing communities work and how to go about setting them up.

McMakin, Jacqueline, with Sonya Dyer. *Working from the Heart: For Those who Hunger for Meaning and Satisfaction in their Work*. San Diego, CA: LuraMedia, 1989. A holistic, well-organized career-planning workbook.

Meeker-Lowry, Susan. *Economics as if the Earth Really Mattered: A Catalyst Guide to Socially Conscious Investing*. Philadelphia: New Society Publishers, 1988. Offers hundreds of suggestions on how average people can invest money and/or their time in building a new economy in harmony with life-affirming values.

Millman, Marcia. *Warm Hearts & Cold Cash: The Intimate Dynamics of Families and Money*. New York: Free Press, 1991. Explores how money is used in families (of all class backgrounds) to express envy, guilt, attachment, and other complex undercurrents of family life. Filled with anecdotes, very readable.

National Association of Community Development Loan Funds. *Directory of Members and Associates*. Greenfield, MA: NACDLF, 1989. Profiles of 77 community development loan funds. Available for $6.50 ppd. from NACDLF, 924 Cherry St., Philadelphia, PA 19107.

Odendahl, Teresa. *Charity Begins at Home: Generosity and Self-Interest Among the Philanthropic Elite*. New York: Basic Books, 1990. A critique of how elite philanthropy primarily benefits the rich. With many engaging quotes from the author's 140 interviews with funders and advisers to the wealthy.

Packard, Vance. *The Ultra Rich: How Much Is Too Much?* New York: Little, Brown & Co., 1989. A study of the rich, critiquing the effects of unlimited accumulations of private wealth on our society.

Rabinowitz, Alan. *Social Change Philanthropy in America*. New York: Quorum Books, 1990. An analysis of progressive philanthropy in the U.S., including a portrait of social change funders and grantees, analysis of 91 sample grants, and directions for the 1990s.

Ram Dass and Paul Gorman. *How Can I Help? Stories and Reflections on Service*. New York: Alfred Knopf, 1985. A moving exploration of the essence of what it means to help.

Rose, Stephen J. *The American Profile Poster: Who Owns What, Who Makes How Much, Who Works Where, & Who Lives with Whom*. New York: Random House, 1986. A poster and accompanying explanatory booklet depicting income distribution in the U.S. along with demographic factors such as sex, race, and occupation.

Rosenthal, Lois. *Partnering*. Cincinnati: Writer's Digest, 1983. Creative ideas from case studies of people who have shared a variety of property, from tools to cars to homes. Very readably written.

Shames, Laurence. *The Hunger for More: Searching for Values in an Age of Greed*. New York: Random House, 1989. A well-written social commentary appraising the economic values of America of the 1980s.

Sider, Ronald J. *Rich Christians in an Age of Hunger*. Downers Grove, IL: Inter-Varsity Press, 1984. From a Christian perspective, an analysis of global inequality and case for social and personal action.

Slater, Philip. *Wealth Addiction*. New York: Dutton, 1983. A provocative, perceptive and entertaining book analyzing addiction to wealth and how to cure it. Includes eight case studies of very wealthy people and their children.

Starhawk. "Bending the Energy: Spirituality, Politics and Culture." In Plant, Christopher and Judith. *Turtle Talk: Voices for a Sustainable Future*. Philadelphia: New Society Publishers, 1990. An interview with feminist leader Starhawk in which she talks about her vision of a spiritually and politically viable future society.

Trainer, E.F. *Abandon Affluence!*. London: Zed Books, 1985. A well-researched analysis of how major global problems stem from an economic system based in unthinking increase of production and consumption. The author sketches an alternative based on simple lifestyles and economic democracy.

Vanguard Foundation. *Robin Hood Was Right, A Guide to Giving Your Money for Social Change*. San Francisco: Vanguard Foundation, 1977. A delightfully personal, readable book on how and why to fund social change, chock full of interesting graphics and quotes from progressive people with money. Available for $9 from Haymarket People's Fund, 42 Seaverns Ave., Boston, MA 02130.

Wachtel, Paul. *The Poverty of Affluence: A Psychological Portrait of the American Way of Life*. Philadelphia: New Society Publishers, 1989. Examines the psychological underpinnings of our seemingly insatiable desire for growth and our vain attempts to fill nonmaterial needs with material goods. Explores how focusing on the possibilities and pleasures that cannot be bought can at once make our lives happier and our society more ecologically sound and economically just.

RESOURCE LIST

Ashoka: A nonprofit agency that grants one to four years of financial support to individuals in the Third World who are taking creative leadership to solve social and environmental problems. Sponsors of the Ashoka "fellows" receive regular reports on their work. Contact: Ashoka, 1200 North Nash St., Arlington, VA 22209; 202/628-0370.

A Territory Resource (ATR): A public foundation funding social change activities in the Northwest U.S. The foundation sponsors educational events for donors, and provides a supportive community for those who join as donors and members of the board to evaluate and fund progressive organizations. ATR also provides technical assistance to grantees and supports cultural work related to grassroots organizing. Contact: ATR, 221 Lloyd Bldg., 603 Steward St., Seattle, WA 98101; 206/624-4081.

Center for Popular Economics: An institute that educates community activists and the public about traditional and alternative economics. CPE offers week-long summer courses and publishes literature in easy-to-read formats. Contact: CPE, Box 785, Amherst, MA 01004; 413/545-0743.

Community Capital Bank and South Shore Bank: These two FDIC- insured banks focus on lending to promote affordable housing, community organizations and small businesses, especially in minority neighborhoods. Contact: CCB, 111 Livingston St., Brooklyn, NY 11201; 718/802-1212. SSB, 71st and Jeffrey Blvd., Chicago, IL 60649; 312/753-5636.

Coop America: A socially responsible marketplace for consumer goods and services, including health insurance, crafts and foods from domestic and Third World cooperatives. They produce a catalog of products for sale, and a quarterly magazine called *Building Economic Alternatives*, which along with feature articles includes a status report of current boycotts. Contact: Coop America, 2100 M St., NW, Suite 310, Washington D.C., 20063; 1- 800/255-4598.

First American Financial Coop: A national agency that provides low-cost financial planning services to individuals. Contact: FAFC, P.O Box 6419, Colorado Springs, CO 80934-6419; 800/422- 7284, 719/636-1045.

The Ministry of Money (M-M): A ministry for people to deepen their faith and to explore their relationship to money from biblical, psychological and sociological perspectives. M-M publishes a newsletter, holds weekend workshops, and leads "pilgrimages of reverse mission" to Third World countries. M-M also has supported the development of a women's network with its own program. Contact: Ministry of Money, 2 Professional Drive, Suite 220, Gaithersburg, MD 20879; 301/670-9606.

National Association of Community Development Loan Funds: A growing national network of loan funds which lend money to low-income community groups at below-market interest rates. Investors can learn about loan funds in their geographic area. Directory of funds, available for $6.50 from NACDLF, P.O. Box 40085, Philadelphia, PA 19106-5085.

National Committee for Responsive Philanthropy: A network of over 100 alternative funds that raise money (over $100 million in 1989) through pay check deductions from workers. A newsletter subscription is available for $25/year. Contact: NCRP, 2001 S. St., N.W., #620, Washington, D.C. 20009; 202/387-9177.

National Network of Grantmakers: A network of several hundred progressive foundations. NNG holds an annual 3-day conference about progressive funding, and produces *The Grantseeker's Guide*, a substantial directory of progressive foundations alongside articles on fundraising and philanthropy. It is available for $27.70 postpaid from: Moyer Bell Ltd., Colonial Hill, Mount Kisco, NY 10549. Organizational contact: NNG, 666 Broadway, #520, New York, NY 10025.

Partners Project: Assists individuals to "adopt an activist" in the Third World. Someone organizing full-time for social concerns (housing, health-care, human rights, women's rights, and other issues) can be completely supported on only $30 to $50/month. Partners are encouraged to build a relationship through photographs, letters, and visits. Contact: George and Lillian Willoughby, 340 Pine Ave., Deptford, NJ 08096.

Partnership for Democracy: A foundation which assists grassroots efforts for peace, and social and economic justice around the country, through grantmaking and technical assistance. Program planning, fundraising, financial management and organizational development assistance provided by six field representatives. PfD also manages donor-advised funds for donors who wish to establish their own funds ($50,000 minimum). Contact: PfD, 2335 18th St., NW, Washington, DC 20009; 202/483-0030.

Pueblo to People/ Alternative Trade Organizations: A non-profit organization marketing products from peasant, refugee and craftspeople cooperatives in Latin America, and providing information about how Latin Americans are organizing to better their lives. Also, provides information about network. Contact: PtP, 1616 Montrose #4400, Houston, TX 77006; 800/843-5257.

Rapid Response Network: A human rights network that helps protect the lives of people in Central America. The network sends telexes in the members' names to key officials to press for the release of abducted activists. Members receive transcripts of telexes and are billed by credit card ($4-8/month). Contact: New England Central America Network, 42 Seaverns Ave., Jamaica Plain, MA 02130; 617/524-3636.

Re-evaluation counseling (RC): An international community of peer counselors providing theory, counseling tools, and support for people to heal and liberate themselves from growing up in an oppressive society. Participants work individually and in identity groups (e.g., as women, Jews, young people). The RC owning class network offers support groups and workshops for members who own or whose families own significant assets they did not earn. Anyone may subscribe to the owning class journal: Contact Rational Island Publishers, 719 Second Ave. North, Seattle, WA 98109.

Shefa Fund: A public grant-making foundation supporting progressive Jewish renewal. TSF hosts donors' forums and plans to organize "tzedakah" collectives for people to do pooled giving. Contact: TSF, 7318 Germantown Ave., Philadelphia, PA 19119-1790; 215/247-9704.

The Social Investment Forum (SIF): A professional association for socially conscious financial professionals and institutions. Friends of SIF receive Services Guide and newsletter for $35/year. Contact: SIF, 430 First Ave. North, #290, Minneapolis, MN 55401; 612/333-8338.

Tides Foundation: A foundation which promotes creative philanthropy nationally and internationally in six general areas: land use, economic public policy, environment, international affairs, community affairs, and social justice. TF runs a grantmaking program where individuals and organizations may set up donor-advised or "component" funds (a minimum of $30,000 is required). Contact: Tides, 1388 Sutter St., San Francisco, CA 94109; 415/771-4308.

Threshold Foundation: Founded in 1982, Threshold Foundation currently gives away over $1 million a year to projects in six areas: peace, environment, personal and community empowerment, social justice, international development, and arts & media. Threshold is made up of people of wealth who pool their time, talents and money to evaluate and fund innovative projects and who educate and empower themselves through the process of philanthropy. The Foundation members are part of a larger, nation-wide network of over 300 people who meet several times a year to explore together issues about wealth — its impact, responsibilities and spiritual dimensions. Contact: Tides, 1388 Sutter St., San Francisco, CA 94109; 415/771-4308.

20/20 Vision: A peace organization that sends subscribers one postcard a month suggesting a 20-minute (or less) action to take to influence elected officials on important national security decisions. Also has an environmental branch. Contact: 20/20 Vision, 1181 C Solano Ave., Albany, CA 94706; 415/528-8800.

Wealth Counselors: Financial counselors and therapists who work with wealthy people (and advise other financial professionals and therapists) on how to address emotional and technical challenges of wealth. Contact:

- Judy Barber, 3672 Sacramento St., San Francisco, CA 94118

- Joanie Bronfman, 1731 Beacon St., Apt.517, Brookline, MA 02146

- John Levy, 842 Autumn Lane, Mill Valley, CA 94941

- David Tobin, c/o AVA, Box 4584, Boulder, CO 80306

- Thayer Willis, 11830 Kerr Pkwy., Lake Oswego, OR 97035

- Community consulting services: Tracy Gary, 3543 18th St., Box #9, San Francisco, CA 94110

- The Impact Project: Christopher Mogil & Anne Slepian, 21 Linwood St., Arlington, MA 02174

Women's Foundations: The National Network of Women's Funds is a membership organization of about 60 public and private women's foundations, as well as individual donors, promoting the development and growth of women's funds that empower women and girls. Contact: NNWF, 1821 University Ave., Suite 409 N., St. Paul, MN 55104, 612/641-0742.

Several of the women's foundations offer Managing Wealth programs to provide women of different backgrounds (with a minimum $25,000 of inherited or earned money), personal support, technical assistance, and an empowerment perspective, via classes, support groups and conferences. Resourceful Women is coordinating a national women's donor network and a leadership training institute. Contact: Resourceful Women, The Women's Foundation, 3543 18th St., San Francisco, CA 94110, 415/431-5677.

SUPPORT FOR MAKING CHANGE

A basic building block of social change is people getting together to reflect on how wider social conditions shape their personal situations and how to take action with other people for change. We invite you to join the explorations of class and money that are happening now in the U.S. and Europe. See if any of the following groups are available in your area. If not, organize one! If you have trouble finding interested people, or would like a boost facilitating an initial meeting or planning how the group will run, we'd be glad to help. Send a postcard to the Impact Project, and we will help connect the people who contact us, either with each other or with the existing groups we know about, or help in other ways as we can. As well as groups, there are counselors who support people with large financial means to make change. See "wealth counselors" at the end of the Resource List.

Support Groups

Support groups provide a safe place to discuss personal issues, in order to gain insights and make progress towards goals. In order to build trust among members, support groups are usually small (3-8 people), homogeneous (members share the same class background and/or current financial situation) and consistent (groups usually meet at least once a month, with members committing to attend a certain number of meetings). Together, group members choose how to run the meetings. A group might focus on a specific topic each meeting (for example, "what's hard and what's good about our class background." or "how we each feel about our current lifestyle"). Or instead, it might have open discussions based on current issues in members lives (for example, "I was figuring my taxes this week and wondered about doing war tax resistance. Has anyone tried it?). Over time, many groups build from an atmosphere of mutual acceptance and respect into a strong sense of community, as people get to know each other and support each other's growth over time.

For step-by-step suggestions on how to run support groups, see "Keeping Us Going: A Manual on Support Groups for Social Change Activists" in the bibliography, and "Taking Charge of our Money, Our Values, Our Lives: a Guide for Support Groups" available from The Impact Project.

Study Groups

Peer study groups provide structure and stimulation to help members learn more about the world. Over the last two decades, an enjoyable and effective participatory format for study groups has been developed, called "Macro-Analysis Seminars" (meaning, studying the big picture). These seminars are easy to organize because they follow a session-by-session outline and include packets of readings. At each meeting, group members report on what they read (each person has read something different from the packet between meetings — most assignments take 15-45 minutes) and then the group discusses them together. Sometimes members of study groups decide to continue together as action groups, organizing around the issues they studied. Here are some study guides currently available. Write for current price information.

- "Class and Social Change" from The Chutzpah Fund, 21 Linwood St., Arlington, MA 02174.

- "Building A Peace System" from Bob Irwin, 36 Baker St., Belmont MA 02178.

- "Organizing Macro-Analysis Seminars: Study and Action for a New Society" from New Society Publishers, 4527 Springfield Ave., Philadelphia, PA 19143.

Conferences and Workshops

Unlike the above groups, conferences and workshops require only a one-time commitment, and help participants feel the power that comes from larger numbers of people sharing the same concerns. These gatherings are being organized by different groups from a variety of perspectives. Resourceful Women offers a variety of programs for women, including conferences and support groups. The Ministry of Money offers workshops from a Christian perspective, focusing on the biblical, sociological and personal aspects of having money. They also have a program specifically for women. The Shefa Fund offers weekends exploring the meaning of money and Jewish renewal. Many local funds of The Funding Exchange offer both workshops and weekend conferences for people with inherited wealth, where participants choose from a variety of workshops on the personal, technical, political, and funding issues of wealth and social change. Some of these funds also offer women's programs, and help to organize support groups.

See Resource list for contact information.

We strongly encourage you to use these formats to talk with others about class, money, and the assumptions and values of our lives. That's how major change begins — people talking with people. From there, attitudes change, actions occur and the structures of society itself begin to shift. Come join in!

This book was a collaborative venture supported by the following organizations:

The Chutzpah Fund of New Society Educational Foundation: Chutzpah promotes the development of long-term, stable resources for nonviolent social change. Established in 1987, the fund does program work and administers funding in three areas: organizing technical assistance, promoting cultural leadership, and supporting the participation of wealthy people in social change. Contact: 21 Linwood St., Arlington, MA 02174.

The Funding Exchange (FEX) is a national network of alternative foundations dedicated to social change, not charity. With three national grantmaking programs and 15 local funds operating in 24 states, The Funding Exchange network gives away over $6 million a year to progressive grassroots organizations. Community activists representing diverse constituencies have a central role in the grantmaking process. The Funding Exchange receives contributions from a broad spectrum of individual donors. FEX sponsors conferences, workshops and retreats, at which people with wealth share personal, political, and financial concerns, in a confidential and supportive atmosphere.

Issue areas funded are: culture and media, community and constituency organizing, the environment, government accountability and civil liberties, lesbian and gay rights, peace and disarmament, anti-racist work, women's rights, workers' rights, youth and elderly, resources for organizing, and international solidarity work in the regions of Southern Africa, Central America, the Pacific rim and the Middle East. FEX also offers donor-advised grantmaking services.

Contact: FEX, 666 Broadway, #500, New York, NY 10025, 212/529-5300.

Member and associate funds of the Funding Exchange

- Appalachian Community Fund, 517 Union Ave #206, Knoxville TN 37902, 615/523-5683
- Bread and Roses Community Fund, 924 Cherry St. #2, Philadelphia, PA 19107, 215/928-1880
- Chinook Fund, 2412 W. 32nd Ave., Denver, CO 80211, 303/455-6905

- Crossroads Fund, 341 West Diversey Ave. #20, Chicago, IL 60647, 312/227-7676
- Fund for Southern Communities, 552 Hill St., SE, Atlanta, GA 30312, 404/577-3178
- Haymarket People's Fund, 42 Seaverns, Jamaica Plain, MA 02130, 617/522-7676
- Headwaters Fund, 122 W. Franklin Ave., Minneapolis, MN 55404, 612/879-0602
- Liberty Hill Foundation, 1320 C Santa Monica Mall, Santa Monica, CA 90401, 213/458-1450
- Live Oak Fund, P.O. Box 4601, Austin, TX 78765, 512/476-5714
- McKenzie River Gathering Foundation, 3558 S.E. Hawthorne, Portland, OR 97214, 503/233-0271, and 454 Willamette St., Eugene, OR 97401, 503/458-2790
- North Star Fund, 666 Broadway, #500, New York, NY 10025, 212/460-5511
- The People's Fund, 1325 Nuuanu Ave, Honolulu, HI 96817, 808/526-2441
- People's Resource of SW Ohio, P.O Box 6366, Cincinnati, OH, 45206, 513/961-6848
- Vanguard Public Foundation, 14 Precita, San Francisco, CA 94110, 415/285-2005
- Wisconsin Community Fund, 122 State St. #305, Madison, WI 53703, 608/251-6834

Institute for Community Economics (ICE): is a private nonprofit organization that provides technical assistance, training and financing to community based organizations developing affordable housing and gaining community control over land, housing and capital. ICE's revolving loan fund borrows funds from socially-concerned individual and institutional investors and lends funds to community based development projects. ICE specializes in providing assistance to community land trusts, community loan funds and other innovative models of community development. Contact: ICE, 57 School St., Springfield, MA 01105. 413/746- 8660.

The Impact Project (TIP): offers a blend of financial and personal counseling, assisting people to take charge of their money and to balance meeting their own needs with creatively employing their resources (e.g., money, time, vision) to

promote social change. The Impact Project educates the public about social change philanthropy and volunteerism, offering private consultations and workshops for families, foundations, universities, church groups and other organizations. Contact: TIP, Christopher Mogil and Anne Slepian, 21 Linwood St., Arlington, MA 02174, 617/648-0776.